# ENTREPRENEURSHIP BELIEVE & ACHIEVE

DELIVERING TO YOU THE CONFIDENCE
TO JUMP INTO SELF-EMPLOYMENT

Steven Pybrum CPA & MBA

Abundance Publishing

Copyright © Material: All rights reserved. This book all or parts, even small parts, thereof may not be reproduced in another document or manuscript or in any other form, electronic, mechanical, photocopied or otherwise, without formal written permission granted by the publisher.

This publication is designed to provide accurate and authoritative information in regard to the subject matter covered. It contains legal matter therefore you are warned to get proper legal, accounting or financial advice before taking any action described or referred to within. It is sold with the understanding that the publisher is not engaged in rendering legal, accounting or other professional services. If legal advice, accounting advice, tax advice or other expert assistance is required, the services of a qualified, competent professional person in your geographic area should be sought.

10 9 8 7 6 5 4 3 2 1

ISBN: 978-0-9651277-1-4

Library of Congress Control Number: 2023917662

Publisher' Cataloging in Publication

Pybrum, Steven

　Entrepreneurship-Believe & Achieve: Delivering the confidence to jump into self-employment/ Steve Pybrum CPA MBA

　p. cm---(Entrepreneurship ; 1)

Includes Index

LCCN: 2023917662

ISBN: 978-0-9651277-1-4

Business, Entrepreneurship, Self Help, Personal Finance

Copyright ©2024, Abundance Publishing

Post Office Box 23209

Santa Barbara, California 93121

www.growmybusiness.help

All rights reserved, including the right of reproduction in whole or in part in any form

Manufactured in the United States of America

# ABOUT THE AUTHOR

STEVEN PYBRUM CPA & MBA has been a radio talk show host and producer of the radio program "Tax Tips." He has appeared in newspapers, magazines and professional journals in articles on financial planning, tax planning, estate planning, succession planning and net worth building. Steven is a syndicated columnist appearing the nation's largest newspapers and magazines with the column "Business Cents" and "Agri Business Tax Tips." Steven is a tax specialist that studied business organizations, team building, leadership then went on to own a leading management consulting firm for small and medium sized business, Canberra Company-Management Consultants.

Steven provides consulting services to companies and the emphasis of Canberra Company is to do the strategic planning causing a business to grow bigger.

Steven has been writing about technical information for over 45 years. He is quite skilled in taking complex matters and making them easy to understand.

Steven has taught many college courses in the Western United States and is often a guest lecturer for business, finance, real estate and taxation courses.

Steven has appeared as a live guest on over 100 television talk shows and news broadcasts on all of the major networks; ABC, NBC, CBS, CNN, FOX and CNBC. Steve has appeared as a live guest on over 400 national radio interviews, providing information about tax law changes, financial planning ideas and current news reports having to do with consumer spending issues, and the state of the economy for small and medium sized businesses.

Steven hopes that you enjoy this groundbreaking book and that you follow through and start your own business to gain life balance, freedom and independence.

# TABLE OF CONTENTS

**About the Author** --------------------------------------------------------- iii

**Chapter 1:** What is Entrepreneurship? ---------------------------------- 1

**Chapter 2:** The Successful Entrepreneur ------------------------------ 21

**Chapter 3:** The Many Hats of The Entrepreneur --------------------- 37

**Chapter 4:** The Banking Relationship---------------------------------- 67

**Chapter 5:** Self-Awareness and Self-Help ---------------------------- 81

**Chapter 6:** Entrepreneurial Operations: DO SOMETHING! ------- 97

**Chapter 7:** Awareness of the Economy and Economic Climate --- 113

**Chapter 8:** Networking, Branching Out, and Leadership ---------- 129

**Chapter 9:** The Psychology of a Business Owner -------------------- 163

**Chapter 10**: Change is Constant ------------------------------------- 183

**Chapter 11:** How To Purchase a Business --------------------------- 199

**Chapter 12:** Financing, Venture Capital and Private Equity -------209

**Chapter 13:** The Pursuit of Profit---------------------------------- 241

**Chapter 14:** How to Start Your Business --------------------------- 253

**Chapter 15:** Being an Entrepreneur --------------------------------- 275

**The End**-------------------------------------------------------------- 291

**Index** ---------------------------------------------------------------- 293

**ORDER FORM**-------------------------------------------------------- 296

**CHAPTER 1**

# What is Entrepreneurship?

Create your own job. Join the ranks of the self-employed, people who are ambitious, responsible, and able to learn new things.

Most people want to become entrepreneurs, own their own businesses, and control their own destinies, but they don't. Studies show that people do not believe in themselves to run a business. People have fears and doubts about leaving the known and diving into the unknown. These well-known hurdles explain why more people don't graduate and then work for 2 to 5 years in a job, then break out into running their own business.

Some don't have the ability to let go of fears, become responsible, and start your own business. Not just any business; you have to start a business that offers something different, new, unique, convenient, and reliable to a group of targeted customers.

In today's highly competitive business landscape, uniqueness is crucial for the success and sustainability of any entrepreneurial venture. Being unique offers several advantages.

It helps you stand out from the crowd, attracting attention and generating interest from potential customers. Uniqueness fosters differentiation, allowing you to carve out a niche market for yourself, free from intense competition.

Uniqueness also sparks curiosity and word-of-mouth marketing, as people are naturally drawn to novel and innovative ideas. Moreover, uniqueness enhances brand value and recognition, creating a memorable and distinct identity that resonates with customers. Ultimately, being unique sets you apart and increases your chances of long-term success in the dynamic business world.

Follow your passion, follow your interests, or feel comfortable that you are in charge; you set your own work schedule. You design the systems, the procedures, the boundaries, and the rules for your own business.

Your business needs to stand for something and deliver something satisfactory to your customers. Once in business, you have to outfox the competition.

Self-employment is a way to get financially rewarded for what you do. With self-employment you gain your freedom, independence, and the ability to take 25 or more vacation days per year.

Many people find relief by purchasing an existing business. That way, you get one year of free coaching from the old owner. Then, once you have your feet on the ground, you offer a product or service that the public needs.

Buying a business has its advantages. You have to do analysis and careful findings of facts. Due diligence investigations are needed. Once you discover why the business is stuck, then you can, in advance, figure out if you have the tools and the network to fix the problems. If so, buying the business can be a good way to approach entrepreneurship.

You may have to twist, tweak, and adjust the business, your policies, systems, procedures, and your vision of the future. Fine tune the business to make it better and different than anyone else in that business you set sail to become the owner of.

Entrepreneurship is a way to get compensated for what you do. If you work hard and smart, you will build a business that can pay you three times more than the 8-5 job. You feel rewarded because you are getting paid for what you do.

The sky is the limit on what you can earn with a fully developed business.

Though innovation is a big part of growing a business, you do not need to be an innovator to start your own business. You have to understand the industry you are operating in, the business practices of that industry, and the Federal, State, and County laws that regulate that industry. Find out who your closest competitors are and study them thoroughly. What products or services do they offer? Which market segment do they service? How content are their customers?

Over time, you will have to polish your skills in accounting, bookkeeping, production, supervision, marketing, advertising, legal, insurance, public relations, leadership and management, payroll tax and income tax issues, and related record retention requirements.

In the marketplace, there are two schools of entrepreneurship. One school is where individuals want to start their own business. The other school is where there are management teams in large companies that want to grow their business by introducing new products and sharpening the existing products so their usefulness and performance reflect the quality of the brand. This is a different type of entrepreneurship.

Large corporate entrepreneurship refers to the process of fostering entrepreneurial initiatives within an established, often bureaucratic, organization. It involves creating an environment that encourages innovation, risk-taking, and agility.

In contrast, regular entrepreneurship typically refers to individuals starting their own businesses from scratch. While both involve taking risks and pursuing opportunities, large corporate entrepreneurship involves navigating existing structures, accessing resources, and dealing with internal complexities, whereas regular entrepreneurship often involves more autonomy and freedom in decision making and resource allocation.

This book is going to be aimed at individuals who want to start a business. How to let go of your fears. How to jump in. How to survive, achieve, accomplish, and flourish.

The largest motivating factor is as follows: it's the tax angle!

If you work for a large company, you could work your way up to manager or vice-president, earn a salary of $200,000, which sounds nice but what you take home is less due to tax withholding: Federal tax of $44,000, State tax of $10,000, and social security Medicare tax of $10,800 you work hard under pressure and the scrutiny of upper management then out of a $200,000 salary you take home $129,168. Salaried employees under current tax law are not allowed any income tax deductions for their salaried business expenses.

## Salaried Employee

| | | | |
|---|---|---|---|
| Salary: | $200,000 | $100,000 | $50,000 |
| Federal Withholding | $44,000 | $18,000 | $7,000 |
| State Withholding | $14,000 | $6,000 | $2,000 |
| Soc Security & MED | $12,832 | $7,650 | $3,825 |
| **Total Withholding** | **$70,832** | **$31,650** | **$12,825** |
| Net Take Home | $129,168 | $68,350 | $37,175 |
| Monthly pay | $10,764 | $5,696 | $3,098 |

There could be additional state and local taxes in your city. This gives you the picture. What after-tax dollars are available to pay rent, buy groceries and gasoline, and other household, entertainment, leisure, and family costs.

## Self-employed Entrepreneur

| | |
|---|---|
| Gross Income | $300,000 |
| Cost of Goods Sold | $105,000 |
| Gross Profit | $195,000 |
| **Business Expenses** | |
| Home Office | $4,080 |
| Car | $14,250 |
| Travel | $18,600 |
| Rental Car | $2,560 |
| Supplies | $10,225 |
| Telephone | $2,450 |
| Internet | $1,425 |
| Computer Supplies | $2,425 |
| Insurance | $4,250 |
| Business Rent | $3,210 |
| Business Land Line | $3,210 |
| Repairs Maintenance | $4,225 |
| Advertising | $3,895 |
| Meals | $3,655 |
| Office Expense | $2,850 |
| Continuing Education | $2,462 |
| Total Deductible Expense | $83,772 |
| Business Net Income | $111,228 |
| Soc Sec Tax | $17,018 |
| State Tax | $1,972 |
| Income Tax Fed | $8,469 |
| **Total tax for year** | **$27,459** |

In doing the analysis first, you can see quickly that the self-employed person could deduct a full range of expenses related to the business. If you look at the salaried employee, they were able to deduct zero expenses, including no car, no cell phone, and no printer.

The salaried person paid a total of $70,832 in total taxes on a salary of $200,000. The self-employed person with a similar salary paid total taxes of $27,495 in taxes. So, you be the judge who got the better deal, the salaried person or the self-employed person?

When I saw this, I chose self-employment.

## Entrepreneurship

Entrepreneurship is difficult to spell and hard to pronounce, but it means job freedom, the ability to be independent, not having to answer to a supervisor, no one is watching, and the flexibility to conduct your day and spend your time in any way that you want to. You can be your own boss.

The term "entrepreneur" likely comes from the French word "entreprendre," meaning to start something. Richard Cantillon, an 18th-century Irish-French economist, is widely credited with defining entrepreneurship — and entrepreneurs — as an economic force that drives development.

The dictionary definition is: one who organizes, manages, and assumes the risks of a business or enterprise.

The term "entrepreneur" has its origins in the French language. It is derived from the French word "entreprendre," which means "to undertake" or "to embark upon." The word was first used in the 18th century by the French economist Richard Cantillon in his book "Essai sur la Nature du Commerce en Général" ("Essay on the Nature of Commerce in General"), published in 1755.

Cantillon defined an entrepreneur as someone who takes on financial risks by combining various factors of production to create and market new goods or services. He described entrepreneurs as individuals who identify opportunities, make decisions, and bear the uncertainty and risks associated with starting and operating a business.

The concept of entrepreneurship was further developed through the works of other economists, such as Jean-Baptiste Say and Joseph Schumpeter, who expanded on Cantillon's ideas. Over time, the term "entrepreneur" has come to be widely used and recognized around the world to refer to individuals who start and manage businesses; innovate, and take risks in pursuit of economic opportunities.

In interviewing CEOs of successful entrepreneurial companies, there is a wide range of advice. One has to be highly focused on the idea, persistent, able to learn about the industry of endeavor, have a vision of how to offer something missing from the marketplace, and know how to get loans. Typically, entrepreneurs are driven and good communicators, place their focus on sales, generate sales, and produce the goods or services to the satisfaction of the customer.

An entrepreneur is swift on foot and flexible.

Further, CEOs of privately held companies doing $500 million per year in annual sales point out the following challenges of an entrepreneur:

1. **Identifying the Product or Service:** First, through good and competent market analysis, you find a slot in the marketplace that needs to be filled. You identify that you have something of value to add to the marketplace. Choosing which business to start is difficult and must be done wisely with the correct calculation so that a herd of customers will come storming through the door to purchase your goods and services.

2. **Scaling and Growth:** One of the primary challenges for entrepreneurs is effectively scaling and managing growth. As a company expands, it becomes increasingly complex to maintain the same level of efficiency and quality. Scaling requires good growth managers, strategic planning, securing additional resources, building

a capable team, and implementing robust processes to ensure sustainable growth.

3. **Competition and Market Volatility:** In today's business landscape, competition is fierce, and market conditions can be volatile. Entrepreneurs need to constantly adapt to changing market dynamics, stay ahead of competitors, and identify emerging trends. Maintaining a competitive edge often involves continuous innovation, market research, and the ability to make agile decisions.

4. **Financial Management:** Efficient financial management is crucial for sustaining and growing a business. You must read, analyze, and understand the balance sheet, the income statement, and the cash flow reports. Entrepreneurs must navigate various financial challenges, including securing funding, managing cash flow, allocating resources effectively, and optimizing profitability. They need to strike a balance between investing in growth opportunities and maintaining financial stability.

5. **Building and Retaining a Talented Team:** A key challenge for entrepreneurs is attracting and retaining top talent. This is a very crucial step. Build a team of top performers, reliable, dependable people with a good work ethic. Building a skilled workforce that aligns with the company's vision and culture is essential for long-term success. Entrepreneurs need to invest in effective recruitment strategies, provide competitive compensation packages, foster a positive work environment, and offer opportunities for growth and development. Then, begin training and retraining employees to perform at a top level while preserving and maintaining the company's integrity, core values, and business reputation.

6. **Risk Management:** Being an entrepreneur inherently involves taking risks. Entrepreneurs must assess and manage various types of risks, including financial, operational, legal, and reputational

risks. They need to develop risk mitigation strategies, implement proper governance structures, and stay compliant with relevant regulations to safeguard the company's interests.

7. **Innovation and Adaptation:** Entrepreneurs must continuously innovate and adapt to changing market demands and customer preferences. They need to foster a culture of creativity, encourage idea generation, and embrace new technologies and business models. Staying ahead of the curve requires a proactive approach to innovation and a willingness to challenge the status quo. You may have a good line of products today, but you have to keep up with the competition, continue to improve your products, add new products, and stay in tune with changing market conditions and changing customer preferences and desires.

8. **Time Management and Work Life Balance:** The demanding nature of entrepreneurship often leads to long hours and high levels of stress. Balancing work and personal life can be challenging, and entrepreneurs need to prioritize their time effectively. Establishing boundaries, delegating responsibilities, and maintaining personal well-being are important to sustain long-term success.

Note that long hours may be part of the first few years, but things get easier over time, and then you can find more time for family, recreation, and vacation.

These challenges, while demanding, can also provide entrepreneurs with opportunities for growth and success. Overcoming these obstacles requires a combination of strategic thinking, resilience, adaptability, and a relentless drive to achieve the company's goals.

## There are three main types of entrepreneurs:

The Creator, The Builder, and The Operator

The creator and the builder are found in small and medium-sized companies. Then, big businesses that talk about entrepreneurship but never become frightened about survival have entrepreneurial lingo; they are usually the best operators and managers of businesses. With their corporate structure and capital access, they can quickly expand a business or product.

In the world of entrepreneurial business, three key roles come together to drive success: the Creator, the Builder, and the Operator. The Creator is the visionary, the dreamer who sparks the initial idea and conceptualizes the business's unique value proposition.

They possess the imagination and innovation necessary to identify opportunities and craft a compelling vision. The builder is the executor, the master of turning ideas into reality. They possess the strategic mindset and leadership skills to design and construct the business infrastructure, assembling the right team and resources.

The Operator is the driver, the person who ensures smooth day to day operations and maximizes efficiency. They possess the practical expertise and adaptability to navigate challenges and steer the business towards growth. Together, these three roles form a harmonious trifecta, propelling the entrepreneurial venture towards more success.

The roles of The Creator, The Builder, and The Operator are vital pillars within the realm of entrepreneurship, each playing a distinctive and crucial part in the journey of a successful venture. The emphasis is that recognizing and embracing these roles can significantly enhance an entrepreneur's ability to navigate the dynamic landscape of business innovation.

The Creator embodies the visionary spirit that propels entrepreneurship forward. Innovating and ideating, Creators conceptualize groundbreaking ideas that form the foundation of new ventures. Their ability to identify market gaps, anticipate trends, and envision transformative solutions is the driving force behind disruptive innovation.

The Builder, on the other hand, translates these visionary ideas into tangible reality. With a focus on strategic planning and execution, Builders design robust business models, secure funding, and assemble teams. Their expertise in creating structures that can withstand market challenges is pivotal for converting concepts into viable enterprises.

The Operator excels at optimizing and scaling operational processes once a venture is established. These individuals ensure efficient day-to-day operations, manage resources and adapt strategies based on real-time feedback. Their attention to detail and ability to navigate complexities sustain the longevity and growth of the business.

The Creator, The Builder, and The Operator are symbiotic roles that drive entrepreneurship's success trajectory. By acknowledging and cultivating these roles, entrepreneurs can harness their combined strengths to forge innovative paths, construct resilient business frameworks, and efficiently steer their ventures toward sustained growth and impactful market presence.

While there is no magic formula for being a successful entrepreneur, those who do succeed tend to have mastered the following set of skills: good and effective communication; being able to sell both themselves and their idea or product; strong focus on the goal; eagerness to learn and flexible; and have a solid business plan.

Intense goal orientation is the characteristic of every successful entrepreneur. They have a vision, and they know how to get there. Your ability to set goals and make plans for your accomplishment is a skill required to succeed. Plan and achieve, then plan and achieve, then plan and achieve more—because without this, failure is guaranteed.

The entrepreneurial mindset combines several different skills that require careful development to successfully achieve a business idea. For example, an entrepreneur must be able to balance an understanding of how business works — including from a financial and operational perspective, with a drive for product perfection and future innovation. Entrepreneurship means understanding when you have an opening in the marketplace that no other provider is meeting and having the business sense to know how to go after this new opportunity at the right time.

A successful entrepreneur will possess many abilities and characteristics, including the ability to be:

- Curious
- Flexible and adaptable
- Persistent
- Passionate
- Willing to learn more
- A visionary
- Motivated
- Focused on the Goal

Entrepreneurial drive stems from qualities like these, just as an entrepreneur's ability to succeed will depend on developing these skills and abilities.

Chapters can be written about the entrepreneur's personality and character profile. We know who the good entrepreneurs are because they survived and ended up with a company with over $500 million in annual sales.

In general, after profiling entrepreneurs, we find that entrepreneurs have a tendency to be:

| | |
|---|---|
| Risk acceptors | Adventurous |
| Disruptors | Independent/Independence |
| Understand professionalism | Freedom |
| Comprehend challenge | Flexibility |
| Overcome their fears | Good workload jugglers |

Able to go from step one to step two, then on to step three

Cash flow scientists

Entrepreneurs can take an idea, build upon it, and add another product, cultivating harmonious products fitting the needs of the customer base

- Emotionally sturdy
- Persistent
- Think on their feet
- People with vision
- People who are multi-talented, multi-taskers

Entrepreneurs can organize, systematize, set policies and procedures, develop methodology, create team players, and possess a sense of purpose aimed at a specific target.

Unruly and undisciplined people do not usually make good entrepreneurs. The disrupter that is unruly and undisciplined is not likely to succeed. People who are averse to risk, people who need certainty and security, and people who do not believe in themselves do not make good entrepreneurs.

In the realm of entrepreneurship, several key roles contribute to the success and growth of a business venture. These roles are vital in navigating the complex landscape of innovation, market disruption, and sustainable business development. Business Schools emphasizes the significance of these roles in its entrepreneurship curriculum.

**Founder/Entrepreneur:** The driving force behind the venture, the founder identifies opportunities, develops a vision, and takes calculated risks. They create a culture of innovation and resilience, setting the tone for the entire organization.

**Co-Founder/Team Members/Executive Suite:** These people are collaborators who bring diverse skills and perspectives to the table. Executives share the workload, responsibilities, and decision making. A balanced team ensures a comprehensive approach to problem solving. Every company needs to have recruiting teams that look for good people to invite onto your company's team.

**Investor/Venture Capitalist:** Financial backers who provide capital and expertise in exchange for equity. Investors play a pivotal role in fueling growth, connecting entrepreneurs with networks, and offering strategic guidance. Investors are usually people with experience and connections within your industry.

**Mentor/Advisor:** Experienced individuals who provide guidance, share insights, and offer valuable feedback. Mentors bring wisdom and industry knowledge to help entrepreneurs navigate challenges and seize opportunities. Maybe an uncle, neighbor, family friend, or someone who has been there and done that before can bring keen insights into your company's direction and the choices you make.

**Innovator/Intrapreneur:** Individuals within established organizations who drive innovation by applying entrepreneurial principles. They identify new markets, develop disruptive products, and foster a culture of creativity. They have a keen awareness of the marketplace and changing trends.

**Strategist:** Professionals who formulate the business plan, set goals, and create a roadmap for success. Strategic thinkers align the venture's activities with its mission, ensuring efficient resource allocation. Strategic planning skills are a must.

**Marketer/Sales Specialist:** Experts responsible for positioning the product or service, identifying target markets, and creating effective sales strategies. They communicate the value proposition and establish a strong brand presence. Marketing is a crucial role in a company's success.

**Operations Manager:** Efficiently handles day-to-day operations, supply chain management, and logistics. This role ensures the smooth execution of business activities and maintains high quality products/services. The whole production area needs high level managers who watch out of many port holes to navigate the choppy waters and provide the necessary supplies to make the product on time and within budget.

**Legal/Financial Advisor:** Ensures compliance with regulations, manages legal matters, and handles financial aspects. These advisors protect the venture's interests and maintain transparency in financial operations. It is key to hire outside law firms to watch the many facets of the business. Government regulations, labor laws, contract law, industry law, product liability, and a host of many more legal fronts you must protect.

In a university's entrepreneurial ecosystem, these roles are studied extensively to prepare future leaders who can navigate the intricacies of business creation, growth, and sustainability. A strong understanding of these roles equips entrepreneurs with the skills needed to drive innovation, disrupt markets, and build successful enterprises.

## What Is Entrepreneurship? / 17

McDonald's Corporation, known for its American hamburgers and the home of the Big Mac, is complimented for its entrepreneurship in taking a simple idea and developing operating procedures and speed kitchens with modern equipment for their franchisees to follow the laid-out systems and procedures for serving customers a quality, uniform product.

McDonald's is somewhat celebrated as the business that proved the concept of franchising. The company was built on some basic principles: quality, service, uniformity, cleanliness, and value.

Their CEO was persistent. They built a product and delivered the product to the customer at a reasonable price.

In order to do this behind the scenes, they needed managers, equipment, and cooperative, dependable, reliable vendors and suppliers. They needed employees and franchisees.

It started as a simple product that was made in southern California by a family that was visited by a salesman of milkshake machines. The salesman saw the product and the interest of the customers and ended up buying the company.

The salesman took the idea back to Chicago and then commenced selling franchises as a way to grow the company. For many years, McDonald's had a combination of company owned stores and eventually drifted toward being a pure Franchisor, with most of their outlets now owned by franchisees.

Proof that the concept of franchising can work. As a franchisee, you can gain permission to have multiple outlets; thus, McDonald's has many franchisees with 30 or more stores.

Here is some incentive: 30 McDonald's stores take 20 years to develop, and then they are able to be sold for $75 million. This might provide a good retirement fund, possibly at an early age.

McDonald's is the world's leading global food service retailer, with over 38,000 locations in over 100 countries. Approximately 93% Of McDonald's restaurants worldwide are owned and operated by independent local business owners.

This milkshake salesman was Ray Kroc, a man driven to grow the company because he believed in the product and then adopted systems, procedures, products, and purchasing power to make it easier for the franchisee to operate their store.

The franchisor delivers the advertising, improves the product through test kitchens, and continues to update the stores, equipment, and design. The franchisor is in charge of developing and changing the product, procedures, and advertising of the product, driving customers to the store, and, in turn, collecting a royalty. The company also charges, based on sales, a fee for marketing and advertising.

The franchisee bears the risk of ownership as they have to order inventory, protect the inventory from theft, put the food into production without spoilage, theft, or waste, refrigerate the product correctly, and serve food to the customer that fits the company's definition of quality and uniformity.

Here is a fine example of entrepreneurship where one side needs the other side to function properly, and by way of this partnership, the product is delivered to the customer.

Entrepreneurship many times has the single owner structure at the outset. There are many different legal entity choices to choose from.

Each business has a different personality and culture. Some of these owners are the "do it my way" kind of heavy-handed disciplinarian, that people hate to work for.

This free-spirited person left the corporate job, bought a business, and then successfully developed the business into more than $10 million in annual sales. One has to question whether this business is running at peak performance. Is this company poised for growth? The answer is no.

Many times, it is the hard work of the consultant to tell the owner, so fixed in their ways, to step aside because the negativity they generate is not conducive to further growth and development of the company. The product is selling, but the employees and the vendors don't like the owner and their poisoned personality.

This style of company needs to have "professional management" that will come in and first make the employees happy, so they will feel good about their work and then the employees will tell other people this is a great place to work. The difficulty in finding employees that the old owner/manager was experiencing goes away. Employee morale improves, and this effervescence shines through to the customer. If the employee is happy and cheerfully greeting the customer, the customer feels appreciated and forms a desire to come back for more products.

Now let's train the staff to become obsessed with serving the customer. Let's talk about growing the company in the direction of the demographic that fits the target market. By doing this, new stores are located well and convenient for the customer profiled to be the consumer who can buy products when needed, driving up annual sales at the clip of 40% per year.

Many entrepreneurs that try to expand do not understand the principles of expansion. Then, after expanding, sales do not go as expected. The entrepreneur becomes frustrated and thus will not expand anymore. Expansion has to occur after careful analysis and then locating the new stores in customer convenient locations.

We see here that the stubborn old cuss that bought the business and grew it to a reasonable size when persuaded to step aside still retained 100% ownership of the company. By contract, he promises not to come around headquarters for more than two hours a week and is prohibited from entering any of the other company stores. When stepping aside and turning things over to professional management, this person now owns a company doing $80 million in annual sales.

This is a hard concept for business owners to comprehend. Most businesses with this style of ownership just keep doing what they are doing with the hardnosed old cuss and not being able to grow sales because of the poor structure, theme, mood, culture, tone, and environment they create.

**CHAPTER 2**

# The Successful Entrepreneur

To be a successful entrepreneur, which business do you enter?

The directory of entrepreneurship possibilities is as thick as the old "Yellow Pages," previously referred to as the phone book. The phone book finally disappeared around 2004 with the advent and reliability of Google and other search engines.

Entrepreneurial businesses are from biotechs to computers to software, retail, service businesses, printing shops, and hair salons—there are at least 1,000 different types of businesses that can be started by you or purchased from a business broker. There is a lot of opportunity here. It is a big country with a lot of underserved people.

Keep in mind Facebook, Microsoft, Google, UBER, Airbnb, Stripe, Doordash, Instacart, Instagram, Moderna, Apple, Tesla, Berkshire Hathaway, Virgin Companies, Charles Schwab, and the list could go on, were all start-up companies, put together by one owner and then blossomed into multi-national companies. You can do this for yourself also.

There is no limitation in entrepreneurship. This is the scary part for most people. No excuse is good enough to prevent you from becoming an entrepreneur or a serial entrepreneur. There is something here for everyone.

Most of the time, in starting a business, you just have to take something and then improve it. To become multi-national, you have to dominate the market. Take a look at In-N-Out Burger and White Castle. They both entered the market when there were already thousands of hamburger restaurants. They simply made a better product that the consumer responded to.

One can lower the chance of business start-up failure and increase their success rate by hiring a consultant to assist with plans and strategy on how to start, how to choose, how to manage and operate, then how to increase the sales of the business. With solid professional help, you will lessen the national statistics about failure. You should make a plan to succeed. Let success be a part of the formula that you follow.

When you commit to being successful and hire a consultant to be there for you when needed, you must carefully follow the steps that the consultant lays out for you. The steps might feel uncomfortable, it does not matter, the key is to follow the steps laid out by knowledgeable people.

Many people hire consultants; the consultant tells them precise steps to take, and then the business owner does not follow the steps because all of this is new to them.

Once you fail to follow the steps to things that you have not done before that seem new and different, the more you resist, the closer to failure you go. So, listen and follow the steps. If you don't understand why, ask the consultant who will tell you to do this because it leads to the next step, leading to higher sales. Be sure to get on the path and follow the steps.

This newcomer resistance is what leads a business to fail. More than 75% of new businesses do not hire consultants to assist them in getting the project off the ground. Of the 25% that hire consultants, 40% refuse or don't follow the steps to success laid out for them.

Entrepreneurs fail because they don't know or understand the self-employed environment, the methodology, systems, and procedures of a successful business. This is evidenced by the fact that they have never owned or operated a free and independent business before.

Many bankers would be bold enough to say that newcomers do not know what they are doing. They violate well established rules. They develop a business plan and profess they are following it, failing to understand that their chief duty is to create new sales. Their chief responsibility is to end the month with a profit.

To become successful, having a friend or relative who has run the same or similar business is helpful. In an undisciplined way, they can tell you the steps they took to success.

You want to be on the right road. You want to take the steps to success. The big problem is that you have never done this before, so you don't do things that you don't know how to do very well. A friend or relative can reinforce what you have to do to keep your head above water. The consultant can give you more precise steps and tirelessly explain why you must take these steps to join the path of success.

The path is clear. Here are the steps. You have to do each of the steps one by one:

- Develop your idea, which becomes your opportunity.
- From the opportunity, you create a business plan.
- From the business plan, you investigate capital needs and secure funding,
- After funding, you go into launch mode.
- From launch mode, you get busy growing the company.
- After some time, you create an exit plan: how do you retire in style?

Developing the business idea is a difficult step. After you talked yourself into becoming or pursuing self-employment, you meet the hard task of deciding what business to start.

If it does not come clear to you, there are some college level courses that you can take where many people in the room are in the same boat. The instructor, by way of lecture, visits with many types of opportunities. You then prepare and pitch your idea to the group to get feedback. In the end, you either go forward with your own crafted idea or adopt an idea that you heard in class and pursue that one. I have seen people switch from restaurants to exercise video courses and many other course corrections.

Now you have chosen an idea, this becomes your opportunity to shine. You have to dig in and make this pursuit successful. You will need an open mind and the desire to make it work.

With your opportunity in mind, you have to create a plan in writing. The plan can be your operating plan, or it can be the more traditional business plan to attract lenders, family, friends, and investors to secure the capital.

Once funded, you can wisely move forward. You have to have securely in mind how you are going to produce the product or service, and then you have to be an athletic track star, never look back, go forward into the world, and attract customers to the business.

You can do this through human contact, networking, or a marketing method that works to gain customers in your industry. There are many software products available to help you with this process. Having good CRM software will be quite helpful.

Filling the sales funnel involves systematically attracting, engaging, and converting potential customers into paying clients. At the top of the funnel, awareness is generated through targeted marketing efforts, drawing in a diverse audience in need of your product or service. As prospects move down the funnel, nurturing strategies like valuable content, personalized communication, and addressing pain points maintain their interest.

The sales funnel process is a structured data path, wide at the top and narrow at the bottom, where potential customers names follow, while the prospect is progressing from awareness to interest, decision, and ultimately, purchase. Marketers use it to guide prospects through stages, optimizing conversions into purchases.

Through the sales funnel, this process, leads gradually to transforming qualified persons into qualified prospects who exhibit genuine intent to purchase. Ultimately, effective sales tactics are employed to guide these prospects toward making purchasing decisions, converting them into loyal customers. A well optimized sales funnel ensures a steady flow of potential clients, fostering business growth and success.

Next, you spend 8 to 10 years developing and growing the company. Growing a management team. Your lieutenants are going to be responsible and in charge of certain aspects of the business, who report to you.

It is your task to do good things to bring life, growth, and consumer appeal to your product or service.

After the passage of time, you can stand back and admire what you have built and measure whether you have been able to scale the mountain to the top. Did you reach the top, or did you just sit down and become complacent halfway up the trail?

With the passage of time and the growth of the company, you have developed something of value. You have to search your soul to determine what you are going to do with this business that you have built. You can sell the business, you can give the business to your son or daughter, or you can make other choices. It's up to you to create an exit plan that will allow you to retire in style.

I have seen it over and over again where people within ten years have developed a sizable business. They sell the business and go into a state of retirement, or they look for the next business to start, grow, and sell. You have the freedom to choose; it's your life, it's your financial future you are building. Let your legs take you as far as you can go. The only limitation becomes you, yourself.

In starting a business, here are some of the things that a person looks for:

Identify the competition, the people in your target area that do the same or similar; you need to know who they are, what they do, and if you bring something better to the table.

Evaluate your idea and assess the market to see if you have concluded that your product or service is a correct fit for this market. Maybe you are a better fit for a larger or smaller geographic market area?

Begin to develop on paper a business strategy. How are you going to roll out the business? How much capital will you need? How are you going to roll out the business with the capital that you have? Some people with the spirit and enthusiasm to be successful figure out how to navigate the early stages, with the access to capital they have, and then execute this plan well.

Study the funding of the business. Sometimes, entrepreneurs are seeking millions of dollars from venture capital firms. Other entrepreneurs are using credit cards and local banks to gain funding. Then, you can also check out the many opportunities for funding available to new start-up companies. Some are community grants, some are state grants, and there are a number of Federal opportunities to get funding. Then there is crowdfunding; seek out the crowdfunding source that is the best fit for your industry. Then, there are family, friends, and grants from private and public charitable foundations.

Seek out someone already in the same business. Interview someone in a distant city who is already in this business. They possibly will answer any questions that you may have. Normally, businesspeople reach out to help new entrants to self-employment once they know you are not the competition. Continue doing this until you have at least two different business owners who will take your call from time to time as you ramp up your business enterprise.

Organize your website, web developer, SEO specialist, and social media accounts so they are ready to announce the launch of your products. Some businesses have gotten off to a roaring start, just priming the pump through social media.

Know that marketing is your most important first step. You have to immediately bring in business and new customers and develop a flow of traffic that will ring the cash register or impress your banker. You will need to have your production infrastructure in place to be able to produce the orders that you secure.

Know that execution is the next most important step. You can execute better from a well-laid-out "operating business plan." The operating the business kind of business plan is different from the business plan used to attract banks, investors, or venture capital. In this plan, you will have mapped out the various steps and timing of steps and events that will help the business launch and move forward.

Don't overlook entrepreneurial incubators. These are places in many cities around the country that are established for the purpose of helping businesses launch. It is a friendly surrounding that is full of people who are consultants or experienced businesspeople who can help get your business started. Once well underway, you can leave the incubator and then occupy your own space with your own equipment.

Business incubators provide start-ups and early-stage businesses with the support and resources that young companies find difficult to access. Their support might involve access to networks, investors, mentors, or co-working space alongside other businesses and experienced professionals.

Similar incubators are designed for bakeries, restaurant operators, or specialty food makers. These are places that have all the equipment to make the product, and they have an avenue and lists of potential customers for your business. They have a delivery method pre-installed. These have proven to be good launch pads for food service businesses.

Get ready to learn. Learn, baby, learn! There are many topics that you will need to know more about. Greet this idea with open arms and continue learning each year you own a business. Learning is a lifetime event. Never quit learning. Sharpen the edge to bring your business to the cutting edge of your industry.

For those struggling to find an idea to latch onto to start a business, many colleges and universities have entrepreneurial courses and classes tuned up to review the possibilities from your solo own business to franchises and then the ups and downs of purchasing a business. These courses are designed to wake the entrepreneur up in you; in the class, you might find your next business partner as there are reports of great medium-sized businesses consisting of two or three owners. When asked where they met, the answer was in the university's entrepreneurial program.

Capital is the second most important step after marketing. Having sufficient capital to start, grow, develop, and expand the business is an important need. Let's take a look at some of the places available to provide you with operating capital.

The SBA (Small Business Administration) is a governmental agency that grants favorable loans to small and medium-sized non-publicly traded companies.

The US Small Business Administration (SBA) helps Americans grow businesses and create jobs by providing resources and tools, including access to capital, opportunities in Federal contracting, access to entrepreneurial education, and disaster assistance for businesses, homeowners, and renters.

The SBA assists small businesses in four main areas: financing, education and training, government contracting, and providing a voice in policy matters. These programs are aimed at helping entrepreneurs start their businesses and keep them thriving.

The SBA reports that small businesses accounted for 45% of the US economic activity. Their report said, "Without small business, the American economy and workforce would be a pretty wild landscape to imagine."

The SBA is there to provide loans to small businesses. The U.S. Small Business Administration helps small businesses get funding by setting guidelines for loans and reducing lender risk. These SBA backed loans make it easier for small businesses to get the funding they need.

So, how it works is that you find out the parameters and requirements for an SBA loan, then align your business to fit the mold, and then apply to see if you qualify. The SBA does not loan the money to you directly.

Go to a bank familiar with SBA loans. Then, if SBA approves your loan, the US government guarantees the loan that the bank made to you. If you default and become unable to pay the bank, then the US government will pay the bank because of its guarantee. With this promise from the US government, the bank agrees to loan you the money. Each month, you pay the required loan payment to the bank.

In short, the bank makes the loan and then collects from you the loan payments. The US government has guaranteed the bank that it will be repaid. Thus, reducing the risk to the bank in the event the business cannot pay back the loan.

Obviously, SBA is careful who they back and oftentimes requires you to give them collateral, such as your personal residence, to help you remember to pay the loan back on time.

Small businesses in the United States generate about 45 percent of our GDP. There are 31 million small businesses, and they are in every industry, from hospitality, biotechnology, computing technology, manufacturing, software development, professional services to construction, and everything in between.

## Business Advocacy Groups

The NFIB (National Federation of Independent Business) A nonprofit, nonpartisan organization founded in 1943, NFIB represents the consensus views of its members in Washington, DC, and all 50 state capitals.

The NFIB's mission is to promote and protect the right of its members to own, operate, and grow their businesses. The National Federation of Independent Business is America's small-business advocacy association headquartered in Nashville, Tennessee.

The Chamber of Commerce is an organization of business owners and entrepreneurs who promote the interests of their local business community. Chambers of commerce provide access to valuable resources, discounts, and relationships that help businesses save money and market their products. The Chamber of Commerce provides valuable networking opportunities between members in the cities in which there is a Chamber of Commerce office.

You will find there is a local Chamber of Commerce in most towns of size across the US. The US Chamber of Commerce is headquartered across Lafayette Square from the White House in Washington, DC. The Chamber's mission is to fight for and advocate the interests of business and free enterprise before Congress, thus influencing new legislation. They advocate the small businessman's prospective to: the White House, regulatory agencies, courts, the court of public opinion, and governments around the world.

These two advocacy groups help promote and protect the interests of small and medium size business owners and are worthy of your membership dues.

## Team Building

A good working atmosphere can encourage cooperation and mutual support among employees and build a deeper level of trust and understanding, promoting team cohesion and efficiency.

Giving employees a good working environment and atmosphere can indeed promote and improve employees' work performance and dependence on the company. A good work environment keeps employees happy and comfortable, making them more focused on their work and motivated to get things done. A good working atmosphere can encourage cooperation and mutual support among employees and build a deeper level of trust and understanding, promoting team cohesion and efficiency.

You want to go the extra mile and generate a sense of family with the employee base. There are many techniques available to do this. For the most part, you have to reach out to make the employee feel wanted, needed, and appreciated. We are all here for a common cause, and because we work together, we should treat one another as family. Welcome to the family. Employee outings, activities, and picnics help improve the feeling of family.

Team building is the process of creating a team that cohesively works together in unison toward a common company goal. The importance and main purpose of team building is to create a strong team through forming bonds and connections. Creating these bonds through team building is very beneficial to businesses and organizations.

On a team, everyone has a job. The baseball team is often brought into board rooms to explain the purpose and structure of the team. Not everyone can be the coach (manager). The first baseman cannot be telling the third baseman what to do and how to do it. If first base is undermining the third baseman because third base is really the position, they want to play this needs to be addressed. Each person does their job to the best of their ability in unison with the other members of the team to create a winning result.

Team building consultants feel grateful when helping to build "team building" within an organization. They appreciate the privilege of working with numerous organizations across the country, helping them achieve unprecedented success through the power of teamwork.

In today's dynamic business landscape, the ability to foster strong collaboration and cohesion among teams is paramount. The consultant sets out to offer you their expertise and guidance in transforming your organization into a high-performing powerhouse.

You will benefit from a comprehensive approach tailored to your needs by engaging a consultant's services. They will start by thoroughly assessing your current team dynamics and identifying areas for improvement. This will provide valuable insights into the underlying challenges hindering productivity and synergy. It's like taking the temperature of the organization and its culture.

Drawing on their extensive experience, they will design and deliver customized team building workshops and exercises that will engage your employees, promote open communication, and instill a culture of trust and respect. These activities will enhance team bonding and develop key skills such as effective communication, conflict resolution, problem solving, and decision making.

The consultant's programs incorporate the latest research and industry best practices, ensuring your organization remains at the forefront of team development. They will empower your teams to overcome obstacles, adapt to change, and maximize their collective potential.

By investing in team building, you will witness tangible results. Improved collaboration will lead to increased innovation, higher employee satisfaction, and, ultimately, enhanced productivity and profitability. Your company will thrive in a supportive environment where employees feel valued and motivated to achieve their full potential.

Businesses should take advantage of their consultant's expertise and embark on a journey towards a stronger, more cohesive organization. Together, they can unlock the untapped potential within your teams and elevate your company to new heights of success, growth, and prosperity.

## A board of directors may engage a team building consultant for several reasons:

1. **Enhancing Team Dynamics:** A board of directors recognizes that effective teamwork is essential for the success of the organization. They may hire a team building consultant to improve communication, collaboration, and trust among board members and senior executives. The consultant can help identify and address any underlying issues that may hinder effective teamwork, which may hinder the growth of the company.

2. **Resolving Conflict:** Board members may have different perspectives, goals, or personalities, leading to conflicts and disagreements. A team building consultant can facilitate conflict resolution processes, help board members understand each other's viewpoints, and find common ground. By fostering better relationships and mutual understanding, the consultant can promote a more harmonious and productive work environment. Harmony in the C-Suite can help everyone be on the same page, on the same team, doing their roles work with a heightened level of focus to help the company grow and expand.

3. **Enhancing Decision Making:** Company executives often make critical decisions that impact the organization's strategy, operations, and stakeholders. A team building consultant can provide

tools and techniques to improve decision making processes within the office. This may include promoting constructive discussions, encouraging diverse perspectives, and establishing frameworks for evaluating options and reaching consensus.

4. **Building Trust and Alignment:** Trust is crucial among team members as they work together to steer the organization's direction. A team building consultant can facilitate exercises and activities that foster trust building among the employees. By creating a safe and supportive environment, the consultant helps management develop stronger relationships and alignment toward common goals.

5. **Maximizing Company's Effectiveness:** The Company may wish to enhance its overall effectiveness and performance. A team building consultant can assess the company's current practices, identify areas for improvement, and provide recommendations to optimize board operations. This may involve refining meeting structures, clarifying roles and responsibilities, and implementing governance best practices.

6. **Onboarding New Members:** When new employees join the company's C-Suite, it is essential to integrate them effectively into the existing company dynamics. A team building consultant can support the onboarding of executive's process by facilitating orientation and training sessions, introducing new members to existing company employees, and helping the new employees establish relationships and understandings among their team.

Overall, by engaging a team-building consultant, the company aims to create a more cohesive, collaborative, and high-performing team that can lead the organization effectively. Team building is important for the board of directors, the C-Suite personnel and the employee base.

## CHAPTER 3

# The Many Hats of The Entrepreneur

There is an old saying: "Love what you do, and you never work a day in your life." Many entrepreneurs can say this.

Becoming an entrepreneur is a thrilling time in life. You have worked hard and have figured out how to join the ranks of the self-employed. In running a business, the business owner has many different roles to play in the business. This hat juggling continues until such time as growth kicks in when you can delegate these tasks to the department head. Then, you can step back and do more important tasks that lead the company onto the path for further growth. Here are the different departments every business has to have.

Beyond these important departments within every business, here are some additional things to consider.

As a beginning business owner, you often have to take on multiple roles and wear many hats to ensure the success of your venture.

**Entrepreneur:** As a business owner, you need to have a clear vision for your company, set goals, and make strategic decisions to drive its growth.

**Manager:** You will need to manage various aspects of your business, including planning, organizing, and coordinating tasks, resources, and people. This involves overseeing operations, setting priorities, and ensuring efficiency.

**Marketer:** Developing effective marketing strategies to promote your products or services, build your brand, and attract customers is crucial. This includes market research, advertising, social media management, and customer relationship management.

**Salesperson:** In the early stages, you may need to handle sales yourself. This involves prospecting, pitching your products or services, negotiating deals, and closing sales.

**Treasurer:** Understanding and managing your business finances is essential for cash flow management. You'll need to create budgets, track expenses, manage cash flow, handle invoicing, and make financial projections.

**Customer Service Representative:** Providing excellent customer service is vital for customer satisfaction and retention. You may have to handle inquiries, address complaints, and ensure your customers' needs are met.

Be sure to inquire with customers about customer satisfaction in person or surveys.

**Human Resources:** If you have employees, you'll need to handle HR tasks such as recruiting, hiring, training, and managing staff. This includes payroll, benefits administration, performance evaluations, and maintaining a positive work environment. In all cases, you will need to have an employee handbook outlining the rules, the boundaries, and the principles that you operate within. You will also need to comply with all employment wage and tax issues with the state and federal government.

**IT Support:** Managing your business's technology needs, including setting up and maintaining computer systems, troubleshooting technical issues, and ensuring data security. You will need to locate suitable software to run the many different functions of the business. Make decisions about what you store on your hard drive and what you let go to cloud or public storage.

**Operations:** The production floor oversees day-to-day operations and optimizes processes to maximize efficiency and productivity.

**Researcher:** Conducting market research, staying updated on industry trends, learning more about every aspect of your product line, and identifying opportunities for growth and improvement.

**Problem Solver:** As the owner, you'll face various challenges and obstacles. Being a problem solver means finding pragmatic or creative solutions, adapting to changing circumstances, and making decisions to overcome difficulties.

**Networker:** Building relationships and networking with potential clients, partners, suppliers, and industry peers can help you grow your business and open up new opportunities.

Remember, as your business grows, you can delegate or outsource certain tasks to focus on your core strengths.

## Accounting

Accounting, you need this because it produces navigation charts and road maps. You need to find out the results of your actions as the owner of the company. There are thousands of small businesses that do not read and refine their accounting systems, accounting procedures, and accounting categories to accommodate the needs of their business.

This is like playing golf without keeping score or driving a boat from San Diego to San Francisco without a map, compass, or depth chart.

So why operate your business by the seat of your pants??? Read the financial reports; if they don't make sense, then sit with your accounting chief and tell them what you need to see to put your finger on the pulse of your business.

The financial reports will tell you with exactness how much your sales are and how much was the cost of your sales. These are important pieces of information. Change your data collection procedures until these numbers are stunningly accurate. Then don't stop until you receive reports that make sense to you.

Most businesses want to know the cost of sales based on items or materials sold, then another page to the report are the labor costs involved in making those sales. With your materials cost split from your labor costs, you will know better what to adjust to make a higher gross profit as a manager.

**The accounting math formula that you will need to know is:**

$$\begin{array}{r} \text{Sales} \\ \underline{- \text{ Costs of Sales}} \\ \textbf{Gross Profit} \\ \hline \end{array}$$

Gross Profit – (Overhead, administrative costs, tax costs, interest costs, depreciation) = Net Profit

If you are good in sales but not in math, the above math is essential to running, managing, and growing your business. You must know these formulas.

Every CEO in America is the captain of the ship they are trying to steer. As the captain of the ship, they know that the end results of their efforts are measured in net profit, and they want this to be the highest possible number after several considerations. The board of directors will measure the CEO's worth to the company based on the achieved net profit. Though in the board room net profits is often expresses as, earnings, as in earnings for the quarter.

The board is a handpicked group of non-employee professionals who serve as an advisory team from many different parts of the same industry. They are there as a sounding board to help the CEO attain their goals. The board is sometimes harsh in telling the CEO that the company is off course and that the CEO better fix it.

In running a business, you, too, will have to do your best to earn a profit. It is easier to achieve a profit if you have an exact number or percentage target you are shooting for. You will find in all CEO literature that you need to operate each day with the target in mind. Then, it is required, not optional, that you monitor the numbers to measure exactly how you are doing in reaching your goal of profit. At all times, keep your focus on the target.

Profit for a business can set off a firestorm from people who don't own a business but want to make a fuss and protest. Keep your head down and do your best to achieve the highest profit possible. Once your business is steady and stable, you have purchased all your desired real estate, and funded your retirement savings account, you can choose to share your profits in such activities as charitable giving and community support projects.

Now you have the tools, the understanding of the purpose of accounting, to review historical data and put it down on paper by reporting period so that you can see if you are on course to earn the highest profit possible. This comes from reading and understanding your financial reports it will ensure that your business will remain open and is properly poised for the future.

Feel free to sit with your chief of accounting and from the data, have them create custom reports, handing you information that will be helpful in being a competent manager of your business. The captain of your ship.

Cash on hand reports, cash flow reports, accounts receivable and payable reports will give you a closer look at the important parts of your business.

Accounting is the way a business keeps track of its operations by collecting data and creating essential reports. Accountants analyze the business finances and then create reports for the owner so the owner can make better decisions.

Accounting plays a critical role in running a business. It provides entrepreneurs with a language to communicate to themselves and to others the financial health of their business. By systematically and consistently recording, summarizing, and analyzing financial transactions, accounting enables entrepreneurs to make informed decisions about resource allocation, pricing strategies, investment opportunities, and cash flow.

It helps them understand the profitability, liquidity, and solvency of their businesses, providing a foundation for financial planning, budgeting, and forecasting. Moreover, accounting facilitates compliance with many regulatory requirements, enhances transparency, and supports stakeholder communication. Ultimately, accounting empowers entrepreneurs to manage and control their organizations effectively, fostering sustainable growth and long-term success.

## Marketing

Marketing is all about telling others about your business. It is distinguished from advertising, which is more specific and consists of the placement of ads in bulletins, newsletters, newspapers, coupon directories, and hanging your brand name in front of the people most likely to purchase your products.

Marketing is the overall effort to tell the world about your business. In performing professional consulting services, I would hate to reveal the number of businesses I have entered and soon ask, "What desk or office is the marketing office?"

This usually is met with the reply from the business owner: "We don't have a marketing department." You can be the best at what you do, but your business is going nowhere unless you tell the right people about your products (your target market.)

To explain marketing, advertising and PR I speak of "start-ups" but I know businesses that have been engaged in business for 15 years that would learn something from reading and noting these fundamental principles.

Once these people are serviced and satisfied, the marketing efforts turn to these satisfied customers to encourage them to tell others: family, relatives, and their circle of friends about your business.

Without a distinct marketing function, your business will never go anywhere. Marketing is not an option to wait for one day when you can afford it. Marketing is a day ONE necessity to get the people interested, then use marketing to boost the volume of customers coming through the door.

An important objective of marketing is propelling a company's growth. This can be seen through attracting and retaining new customers.

Companies may apply a number of different marketing strategies where creativity can be used to achieve these goals. For instance, matching products with customers' needs could involve personalization, prediction, and essentially knowing the right problem to solve.

Another strategy is creating value through customer interaction and experience. This will have the tendency to elevate customer satisfaction and remove any difficulties with the product or service. Paving the way for a happy customer to tell others. Connected pieces of marketing are advertising and public relations.

Marketing is a day one function for a start-up business because it creates brand awareness, attracts customers, and generates revenue. From the moment a start-up enters the market, it needs to establish its presence and communicate its value proposition to potential customers.

Early marketing efforts help build a customer base, gather feedback, and refine the product or service based on real world responses. Effective marketing strategies can differentiate the start-up from its competitors, facilitate growth, and secure investor interest. By focusing on marketing from the beginning, a start-up can lay the groundwork for long-term success, establish a strong market position, and create a trajectory for sustainable growth.

Ignoring marketing in the initial stages could hinder visibility, slow customer acquisition, and impede the business's overall potential.

In a start-up business, the interplay between marketing, advertising, and public relations (PR) functions is crucial for creating a strong brand presence, attracting customers, and establishing a positive reputation in the market. While these functions have distinct roles, they often overlap and complement each other in various ways. Here's how they interact:

**Marketing:** Marketing involves a broader set of activities to understand customer needs, create products or services that fulfill those needs, and promote them to the target audience. Marketing includes market research, product development, pricing, distribution, and promotion strategies. In the context of a start-up, marketing sets the overall strategic direction by identifying the target market, customer segments, and value proposition. It provides the foundation for advertising and PR efforts.

**Advertising:** Advertising is a subset of marketing and focuses on paid promotional activities through various channels such as online ads, social media ads, print media, radio, TV, and more. In a start-up, advertising helps generate awareness, drives traffic, and attracts potential customers to the business. The advertising message is designed to be persuasive and attention grabbing, often highlighting the unique features or benefits of the product or service.

**Public Relations (PR):** PR is the practice of managing and maintaining the reputation of a company or brand. PR activities include building relationships with media, influencers, customers, and stakeholders. PR efforts aim to create a positive public image and manage any potential negative perceptions or crises that may arise. In a start-up, PR can help build credibility, establish thought leadership, and enhance brand trust through media coverage, press releases, events, and community engagement. Public relations people can get you free radio, television, and print advertising by using their skills and contacts to update them on certain interesting things or accomplishments of your business.

## The interplay between these functions in a start-up business can be illustrated through various scenarios:

**Strategic Alignment:** Marketing establishes the strategic foundation by identifying the target audience and messaging. Advertising and PR strategies are aligned with this foundation to ensure consistent brand messaging across all channels.

**Integrated Campaigns:** Successful start-ups often integrate advertising and PR efforts to maximize their impact. For instance, an advertising campaign can be supported by PR activities like media interviews, guest articles, or influencer partnerships to increase credibility and reach.

**Content Synergy:** Content created for advertising campaigns can also be repurposed for PR purposes. High quality content can be used to establish the start-up's expertise, provide value to the audience, and enhance its reputation.

**Crisis Management:** When a start-up faces a crisis or negative publicity, PR plays a critical role in managing the situation. Simultaneously, marketing and advertising teams may adjust their strategies to address concerns, reassure customers, and mitigate any damage to the brand's reputation.

**Feedback Loop:** Feedback received from advertising and PR efforts can provide valuable insights for marketing strategies. Customer survey responses, engagement metrics, and media coverage can help refine and adjust the start-up's overall marketing approach.

The interplay between marketing, advertising, and PR in a start-up and a seasoned medium sized business, involves a coordinated effort to create a strong brand presence, attract customers, and maintain a positive reputation. Each function contributes its unique strengths to the overall business strategy. When these functions work harmoniously together effectively, they can lead to increased brand awareness, customer loyalty, and business growth.

## Management

This is the job of the owner of the business. This involves planning for the current day and the future of the business, organizing and running your business without duplicate steps in a precise way so that everyone knows their specific function and performs that function well, and controlling—you are in charge. Don't let the employees be in charge; it is your business. You are the captain of the ship; you call the shots and weed out the bad apples that will not follow your direction.

The basic principles of management are best summarized by Planning, Organizing, Staffing, Directing, Coordinating, Reporting, and Budgeting. If you are actively performing these steps, you are coming close to what an ideal manager would do. Through delegation, you may have additional managers in your business that report to you. They, too, have to be good at planning, organizing, staffing, leading, and controlling.

With ownership comes control. You are in charge of your own destiny. You have to actively participate in ownership steps of planning, organizing, staffing, training, and controlling all functions within the business, ensuring everyone is doing their job. You need to improve so that you are convinced that you are in charge, you call the shots and you run and lead the company, with politeness and dignity.

Then consider from another angle: if you are doing all these steps well, then what is missing? What function is not working to raise sales? What are the remaining steps to be performed?

Notice it is not making a list of what needs to be done. It is a managerial evaluation of what is being done well and what is not being done that will drive new customers in the door. When the current owner is not performing these steps well, it is time to hire "professional management" to come into the business with new energy and incentives to make the business perform well and grow bigger each year.

As an entrepreneur, you cannot stand around and hope things will go better. As the manager, you have to expend energy, apply education, and perform steps that will assist the business in its growth cycle. You have to have the necessary vision of the future and work toward that vision, staying focused on the end target.

If you stand around and watch the water, come into the boat as the captain of the ship; if you continue to let water in, you will sink. A person in second grade can do the analysis and figure this out. As captain of the ship, you need to be on the ready at all times to oversee that people are bailing out the water that came on board while other people are patching the leak. Once the leak is stopped, the people who are bailing out the water will have less to do and can then be redirected by you to perform other tasks.

Too many times as a consultant, I see people running small and medium sized businesses frozen in place, not knowing what to do next, and then soon, the doors to the business are closed.

The multi-tasking entrepreneurial manager is always vigilant, watching and anticipating what needs to be done next to keep the business afloat. Then, what steps need to be taken to get the ship up to racing speed to become competitive and eventually win the race by selling the business for a large fortune?

The management function is crucial for any company, regardless of its size or ownership structure. In the case of a medium-sized privately owned company, effective management becomes even more essential due to several reasons:

**Resource Optimization:** Medium-sized companies often operate with limited resources compared to larger corporations. Effective management ensures that these resources, including financial, human, and technological assets, are allocated optimally to achieve the company's goals.

**Strategic Decision Making:** Management is responsible for making strategic decisions that shape the company's direction. In a medium-sized company, decisions made by management have a direct impact on the company's growth and competitive positioning. Effective strategic decisions can help the company capitalize on opportunities and navigate challenges.

**Flexibility and Adaptability:** Medium-sized companies need to be agile and adaptable to changes in the market, industry, and competitive landscape. Effective management ensures that the company can respond quickly to new opportunities and challenges, essential for sustained success.

**Employee Engagement and Productivity:** Management plays a pivotal role in fostering a positive work environment, promoting employee engagement, and enhancing productivity. In a medium-sized company, each employee's contribution can significantly impact the overall performance, making effective management of human resources crucial.

**Innovation and Creativity:** Management sets the tone for fostering a culture of innovation and creativity. Medium-sized companies often rely on innovation to differentiate themselves and compete effectively in their market niche. Effective management encourages a free flow of ideas and supports the implementation of innovative strategies.

**Financial Management:** For privately owned companies, financial stability is critical. Effective management ensures proper financial planning, budgeting, and cost control. This is particularly important for medium-sized companies that may not have the financial cushion that larger corporations possess.

**Risk Management:** Every business faces risks, and management is responsible for identifying, assessing, and mitigating these risks. In a medium-sized company where there might be less room for error, effective risk management is essential to prevent potential setbacks.

**Customer Relations:** Management plays a role in maintaining strong customer relationships. In medium-sized companies, personalized attention to customers can lead to higher customer satisfaction and loyalty.

**Coordination and Communication:** As a company grows, coordinating different departments and teams becomes more complex. Effective management ensures that communication flows smoothly, ensuring alignment across various functions.

**Long-Term Vision:** While short-term goals are important, management in a medium-sized company must also have a long-term vision. This involves identifying growth opportunities, diversification strategies, and sustainable business practices.

Effective management in a privately owned company is vital for optimizing resources, making strategic decisions, fostering innovation, managing risk, maintaining financial stability, and more. It sets the tone for the company's overall success and growth trajectory.

## Purchasing

The purchasing department will have an understanding of the raw materials you will need to operate your business. The purchasing department is constantly looking for ways to buy higher quality materials at a reduced price. This can be accomplished by promising volume purchases in exchange for preset prices. This is sometimes accomplished by linking or partnering with some business that make the raw materials that you need. There is a specific art to the business of purchasing managers. The art of buying high quality items for less to help make the gross profit go up or increase.

Here are some insights into the responsibilities of a purchasing agent in an entrepreneurial business. The role of a purchasing agent is crucial in ensuring the smooth operation of the business and managing the procurement process efficiently. Here are some key responsibilities typically associated with the role of a purchasing agent.

**Strategic Sourcing:** Purchasing agents are responsible for identifying and evaluating potential suppliers offering competitive pricing, conducting market research for alternate higher quality suppliers, and negotiating contracts. They need to develop and maintain relationships with suppliers to ensure the business has access to quality products or services at competitive prices and timely delivery.

**Supplier Management:** Purchasing agents are responsible for managing relationships with suppliers throughout the procurement cycle. This includes monitoring suppliers' performance, addressing any issues or concerns, and working collaboratively to improve delivery times, quality, and overall value.

**Cost Analysis and Negotiation:** Purchasing agents play a vital role in cost management by conducting cost analysis and finding opportunities for cost savings for the company. They need to negotiate favorable terms and conditions with suppliers, including pricing, payment terms, and contractual agreements while maintaining the quality standards required by the business.

**Inventory Management:** Purchasing agents are responsible for maintaining optimal inventory levels. This has proven to be a critical role within a business. There is some software for certain industries that will help with optimal order quantities to better stock inventory without having an unnecessary investment in inventory items. Just in time inventory system is a management strategy that aligns raw material orders from suppliers directly with production schedules.

Just in time inventory systems, order items with just the right amount of lead time to have items arrive in the manufacturing plant 48 hours before they are needed on the production floor.

Purchasing agents must forecast demand, monitor stock levels, and coordinate with other departments, such as sales and production, to ensure the right quantity of inventory items is available at the right time. Efficient inventory management minimizes the costs associated with having excess inventory or obsolete parts.

The risk management element of purchasing. Purchasing agents (PAs) need to assess and mitigate risks associated with the supply chain. This includes being a visionary by identifying potential disruptions, such as supplier capacity issues, quality problems, or geopolitical risks and tariffs. Also important are the steps of developing contingency plans, identifying in advance the supplier's own company disruptions, and developing a backup plan in the event a supplier is going to fail to deliver. The purchasing agent should stay informed about industry trends, regulations, and compliance requirements to ensure the business remains in compliance with relevant laws and regulations.

There is a continuous improvement element: PAs are responsible for continually evaluating and improving the procurement process. They should seek opportunities to streamline operations, identify cost saving measures, and implement best practices. By staying abreast of industry trends and innovations, they can optimize the procurement function to support the entrepreneurial businesses' overall objectives.

It is important to note that the specific responsibilities may vary depending on the nature of the business, its industry, and the size of the business. Much importance needs to be placed on skills of vision of the future needs, production pipeline, negotiating skills and classes, awareness of legal contracts, and how to add to your existing contract terms and conditions that will assist and protect the business.

An exceptional purchasing agent for a privately owned manufacturing company brings immense value by securing cost effective raw materials, negotiating favorable supplier terms, and ensuring timely deliveries. Their expertise optimizes inventory management, reducing excess stock and minimizing production disruptions. By staying updated on market trends and innovations, they source high quality materials, enhancing product quality. Financially, their strategic sourcing drives down costs, improving profit margins. Moreover, their adeptness in relationship building cultivates strong supplier partnerships. Ultimately, this agent streamlines operations, enhances competitiveness, and enables the company to allocate resources efficiently, fostering growth and sustained success in the dynamic manufacturing landscape.

## Payroll

You will have to decide who is a vendor (independent contractor) and who is an employee, using fairly well outlined standards published by Federal and State governments. Employees need to be identified and categorized based on local labor laws and taxing authorities' regulations, which every employer must read and know about.

Watch for the labor law firms in your area and find out from them when they are going to have their next free seminar. There are other law firms that specialize in representing employees, and their prey is businesses that do not know current day labor laws. In the mix is how you are going to have training classes and deal with sensitive issues like unfair labor practices, sexual harassment, wrongful termination, overtime pay, and a host of other high penalty issues you could encounter if you do not know and understand, as the business owner, the labor laws.

The payroll department issues paychecks to the employees on a schedule and on time. The employer withholds employee payroll taxes and is the trustee of those funds. The employer must pay the correct amount of payroll taxes to the State and Federal government agencies.

The fastest way to have your business doors closed is the failure to collect and remit payroll taxes. So that you do not get into payroll tax problems, it is best to link with national firms like ADP or Paychex to have them process payroll, remit payroll taxes, and direct deposit employee paychecks. You want the payroll department to run smoothly, on schedule, on time, and without huge penalties from State or Federal agencies.

More specifically, the payroll department manages the company's payroll process and ensures that employees are paid accurately and on time. The specific duties and responsibilities of the payroll department typically include:

**Employee Data Management:** Collecting and maintaining accurate employee information, such as personal details, employment status, tax withholding forms, and benefit deductions, and guiding employees to accurately complete the W4 Form and the I-9 Form.

**Timekeeping and Attendance:** Tracking employee attendance, breaks, leaves, overtime, and any other time related information to calculate accurate wages and ensure compliance with labor laws and company policies. Notify employees of pre-tax and post-tax benefits and opportunities.

**Payroll Processing:** Calculating employees' wages, salaries, bonuses, commissions, reimbursements, and other compensation elements based on approved time and attendance records. This involves taking into account deductions for taxes, benefits, and other authorized deductions.

**Payroll Adjustments and Updates:** Processing any changes to employee compensation, such as promotions, salary increases, deductions, or changes in benefits. This includes ensuring that the necessary approvals and documentation are in place.

**Tax Compliance:** Payroll tax tables change at the whim of Congress. The payroll department and its vendor must calculate and withhold the correct amount of taxes from employees' paychecks, including income tax, social security contributions, Medicare, and any other applicable state and local taxes or voluntary deductions of the employee. The payroll department also ensures that the necessary tax reports and filings are submitted to the appropriate government agencies on a timely basis.

**Benefits Administration:** Managing employee benefits programs, such as health insurance, retirement plans, and other voluntary deductions. This includes enrolling new employees, processing changes, and addressing employee inquiries related to benefits. Having a tickler file to alert you that based upon the number of months an employee has been with the company, the new benefits an existing employee is now qualified to receive.

**Payroll Records and Reporting:** Maintaining accurate and up-to-date payroll records, including employee earnings, tax withholdings, benefits deductions, and any other relevant information. Generating payroll reports for management, accounting, and auditing purposes. Keeping and storing the payroll records for the correct statutory periods, satisfying federal and state laws.

**Compliance and Regulations:** Staying informed about relevant labor laws, tax regulations, and employment standards to ensure compliance. The payroll department is responsible for implementing any necessary changes to payroll processes or policies to meet legal requirements. The payroll department must contribute to updates to the employee handbook as needed. Training sessions may be necessary to inform employees about your standards, ethics, and values.

**Payroll Inquiries and Issue Resolution:** Addressing employee inquiries related to payroll, including paycheck discrepancies, tax withholding inquiries, and other payroll related concerns. Resolving any issues or discrepancies promptly and accurately.

**Collaboration and Coordination:** Working closely with other departments, such as HR and finance, to ensure seamless integration of payroll processes with other business functions. Collaborating with external entities, such as payroll service providers or tax authorities, as necessary. Having a clog in the payroll department can contribute to employee stress, morale, and dissatisfaction with the company if the payroll is not treated with care and delivered accurately and on time as promised.

Having an experienced person oversee and manage the payroll department is immensely valuable. Their expertise ensures accurate and timely salary processing, minimizing errors and preventing potential legal and financial issues.

With an understanding of complex tax regulations and labor laws, they guarantee compliance, reducing the risk of penalties. An experienced manager can optimize processes, streamline workflows, and implement best practices, leading to increased efficiency.

Their ability to handle discrepancies, address employee concerns, and communicate effectively fosters a positive work environment. Moreover, their insights contribute to strategic decision making by providing data driven analyses of labor costs and trends. Overall, the presence of an experienced payroll manager promotes smooth operations, enhances employee satisfaction, and safeguards the company's financial stability.

## Innovation

A business will stagnate and then fall behind if you do not have an innovation department. This creative thinking department finds ways to increase your product line with products that will sell faster than your current products. Do not innovate to come up with baggage products that don't complement the main products or sell slower than the main products.

Part of innovation for a small business is connected to the merger and acquisition department. The merger, acquisition, and innovation departments are considered one department in a small and medium sized business framework.

The idea here is to look for struggling competitors who have started an idea, but the target business is not well informed on how to operate their business, therefore making the business a target for you to acquire.

Then, after purchasing the business, you learn how to make their products and add them to your product line. Then, commence selling the product through your product path, to your list of customers, or through outlets where you have shelf space or inroads to display the product so that you can begin increasing your sales in a profitable way.

A wide variety of business industries have brokers or businesses that specialize in selling small and medium size businesses because the owner is tired, retiring, transitioning into a new endeavor, or permanently going on vacation. Whatever the reason, keep your eye on the marketplace for complementary products to increase your sales. Do not be timid about buying out another business.

Innovation is the lifeblood of progress and success. It requires a combination of creativity, problem solving, and adaptability. To thrive in today's dynamic, ever changing business landscape, entrepreneurs must foster a culture of continuous innovation, embracing change, challenging norms, and pursuing novel solutions.

Innovation includes the steps of constantly being on watch patrol for your products that are currently losing favor with the customers and looking for new ways and new products to offer to the customer base.

Remember, innovation is not merely an option but an essential mindset that propels businesses forward and unlocks untapped opportunities. Embrace innovation, and let it shape your entrepreneurial journey. Don't allow your business to fall behind.

## Quality Control

Quality control is another desk and department that is often missing from a business that is small or of medium size. Every business, big or small, has to have a quality control department.

The function here is to check the products you are making. Are they standing up to the test when used by the consumer? What condition is the product in after 36 and 60 months? You have to know this. Is there a part that is constantly breaking? Is there a service that is falling short of being the best in the marketplace? What can you do to be sure the product you are selling is durable and competitive in the marketplace?

When we look at law firms and accounting firms and ask them about quality control, they indicate "not needed." This is an immediate signal that trouble is brewing in this business.

When we enter a brewery to provide consulting services, we check up on their quality control function. Sometimes, this important component is missing. The questions have to be raised: for example, is the beer that won the ribbon the beer that is now being put into bottles and kegs? You can quickly see the need and necessity to spend at least six hours a month evaluating the quality control of the products that you make.

Quality control is paramount in any entrepreneurial business. A commitment to maintaining exceptional standards ensures that customers receive a consistently excellent product, fostering customer loyalty and supporting the building of a strong brand reputation.

In the context of brewing, quality control encompasses numerous aspects, including ingredient sourcing, production processes, and product consistency. By implementing stringent quality control measures, a top brewery can guarantee that only the finest ingredients are used when the process is working, resulting in superior taste and aroma.

Rigorous testing throughout the brewing process ensures that each batch meets the highest standards, minimizing the risk of defects or inconsistencies leading to poor quality. This attention to detail about quality not only enhances customer satisfaction but also safeguards the brewery's reputation in a competitive market. Ultimately, prioritizing quality control in a top brewery entrepreneurial business is essential for delivering an exceptional beer experience and maintaining long-term success.

Having a strong quality control person in a privately owned company is crucial for ensuring consistent product excellence. They oversee production processes, identify defects, and enforce adherence to industry standards.

This leads to improved customer satisfaction, as high-quality products enhance the company's reputation and loyalty. A dedicated quality control professional minimizes the risk of faulty items reaching consumers, reducing potential recalls or customer complaints.

This can result in cost savings by avoiding rework, returns, and legal issues. Moreover, robust quality control fosters operational efficiency by streamlining processes and identifying areas for improvement. It also aids in regulatory compliance, preventing fines and penalties. Ultimately, a proficient quality control person in a privately owned company upholds brand integrity, drives competitiveness, and supports sustainable growth.

## Record Retention

Federal and State laws mandate the keeping of certain records for statutory periods of time. Your insurance company, taxing authorities, banker, satisfying safety standards, or other outside agencies and entities may require you to maintain certain records for a specific period of time.

These records need to be secure and reproducible for up to 7-10 years in some cases. Record retention in the past required a warehouse; today, it may be a computer server in a remote location and backups that you maintain on an appropriate device.

You may have a vendor or service that assists you in record retention. The warehouse is not a bad idea if you fully understand litigation and the rules and procedures of discovery. The hungry lawyer attacking your business may learn about your cloud service and then serve upon the service a subpoena asking the service to turn over all of your records in their governance. The judge will then order that the encryption keys and passwords be turned over to the hungry lawyer.

You need to be aware of this hazard common to the marketplace. The same goes for your email provider. Know that when you send an email and erase it, it is still on the server of your email provider. Please know your provider's policy about total destruction of your sent and received emails to protect you against the hungry litigator!

Record retention is crucial, for example, to wineries due to various reasons. Record retention ensures compliance with regulatory requirements, as wineries are subject to taxes, laws, and regulations pertaining to production, labeling, and distribution.

For many companies, including manufacturing, record retention aids in quality control and traceability, allowing, for example, wineries to track the entire production process, from grape sourcing to bottling.

Additionally, record retention facilitates financial management, inventory tracking, and analysis of consumer preferences, helping wineries make informed decisions and improve operations. Ultimately, it safeguards the winery's reputation and builds trust with customers and stakeholders.

Record retention enhances a company's credibility and integrity by establishing a transparent and organized documentation system. It ensures crucial information, such as payroll records, financial transactions, contracts, and communication, is preserved accurately over time.

This practice fosters accountability, regulatory compliance, and the ability to demonstrate a history of responsible business practices. Clients, partners, and regulator's view companies with effective record retention as trustworthy, as they exhibit a commitment to transparency, accuracy, and ethical operations. This bolstered credibility contributes to a positive reputation and fosters greater confidence in the company's dealings and decision making processes.

## Public Relations

The public relations department can be an internal department or an external vendor, as is your law firm and your accounting firm. The purpose of the public relations department is to get you millions of dollars in FREE advertising by coming up with jingles, songs, and data interesting to newspapers, radio, magazines, television news, and social media outlets.

What you dangle is so interesting that it makes the 5 p.m. news. The news show tells two million people. You get your company or brand mentioned, and the public has heightened awareness of the products that you offer.

This broadcasting of information about your business is FREE. If you purchased a spot in a magazine or three minutes on a news show, it would cost you millions of dollars to place that ad. The cleaver public relations person gets your mentions in the news frequently, at no cost. It takes talent, creativity, and connections to have this happen. Hire the right people who will deliver what they promise while they prove to you that they have done this before.

Social media also offers public relations experts who possess the creativity to come up with social media-friendly pieces of information that cause the consumer to want and order your products. Many cosmetic lines have gone from the garage and have grown into one billion dollars in sales simply by using Instagram for free.

Hiring a public relations (PR) firm can be a game changer for manufacturing companies. In today's competitive market, maintaining a positive public image is crucial. A PR firm brings expertise in managing external communication, enhancing brand reputation, and handling crisis situations effectively. They craft compelling narratives, engage with media outlets, and secure positive press coverage, boosting the company's credibility and visibility.

With their strategic approach, PR firms help manufacturers effectively reach their target audience, build trust, and differentiate themselves from competitors. By managing public perception, a PR firm can contribute significantly to a manufacturing company's success, fostering customer loyalty, attracting investors, and strengthening industry partnerships.

To be an entrepreneur, you have to do all of these tasks, from accounting to public relations. You personally have to be able to wear all the hats until your sales perk up, and you then can afford to delegate these tasks to others.

In starting your business, you have to be performing all of these tasks from day one.

## Basic Operations Framework of a Business

All businesses can be analyzed, scrutinized, and dissected into this operational framework.

45% Production

45% Marketing and distribution

10% Administration, i.e., accounting, bookkeeping, HR department

I hear often this question in business of all sizes. Do you ramp up production first or do you hold off and let the marketing side of the business produce the orders first? This complex question is like a two-sided coin, which is the correct answer?

A business owner can stay awake arguing with their spouse whether you first get well established in production, then you start marketing and distribution. Or do you lead with getting sales orders and then come back to the business and hope you can make the products on time?

The argument can go on for weeks at a time without reaching a conclusion.

In the management consultant's handbook, the best picture of this problem exists in the winery business. There is a country full of good winemakers. They make very good wine and win ribbons. Their winery sells 500 cases of wine per year.

At this sales level, this business has not yet left the hobby stage of the company's life cycle. This business is stuck because no one involved with making the wine knows how to sell the wine or find distribution representation that will help place the wine and the ribbon on store shelves so that the aware consumer will select the product.

The production side of this business is warmed up and ready to make 2000 cases of wine per year, but either they don't, or their banker won't let them. Because the track record is they sell 500 cases per year to their customers. If they produced 2000 cases per year, then 1,500 cases per year would go into storage in a warehouse, hopefully a temperature controlled warehouse.

After five years, they have 7500 unsold cases of wine that are aging fast. The best decision for this business is to sell the excess inventory to "two-buck chuck" while getting paid 10% per bottle of the retail price for the wine. The point is you do not want to be an entrepreneur who makes decisions to make the product faster than you can sell the product. On the other hand, you don't want to accept orders for products that you cannot produce on time in accordance with the terms contained in the purchase order.

While both production and marketing are crucial components of a successful business, the decision to prioritize one over the other depends on the specific circumstances and goals of the company.

Growing production first may be advisable when there is a high demand for the product, limited supply, or the need to improve operational efficiency. This approach ensures the company can meet customer demand and efficiently fulfill orders.

On the other hand, prioritizing the growth in the marketing department can be beneficial when there is an untapped market, intense competition, or a need to raise awareness and drive customer acquisition. By expanding its marketing efforts, the company can increase brand visibility, attract new customers, and ultimately generate higher sales. Ultimately, the management consultant emphasizes the importance of considering the unique context and goals of the business to make an informed decision regarding the sequence of growth.

To understand business, you have to consider the above factors and how they interrelate. You can't have one without the other. Business can bring the most complex set of circumstances that you will ever encounter.

Constant and vigilant review of the pieces of the puzzle is important. The constant question of what is missing what is holding us back from that next breakthrough to growth? With informed decision making, gaining momentum and eventually breaking out into explosive organic growth. This is how you manage a company, by frequently evaluating the business as a whole and supplying the next push in the correct direction to make things better.

This takes us to a place where we can look at the concept of growth company management. With growth comes challenges. Some businesses take off, and management is not prepared for the ride. Things can go sour during an upcycle of growth due to a lack of knowledge and experience in how to manage growth.

Then, you have to hire the right people at the right time with growth company experience. A whole book could be written about the trials and tribulations of managing a growth oriented company. The appropriate title might be "Hang On For the Ride."

The best you can do is to be aware of your circumstances at all times and know when to bring in some knowledgeable outside help. This does not mean calling the bookkeeper to see if they know anything. It means bringing in a consulting firm with growth company experience that can steady the wild bull while you go for a ride and come out the other side with a company that has grown beyond your wildest imagination.

CHAPTER 4

# The Banking Relationship

Having a good business working relationship with you banker is very important to you and for the health of your business.

## The Banker

Well, Johnny, you thought by becoming an entrepreneur that you were going to be your own boss. Well, guess what? Self-employed people have a boss—it is their banker. The banker will tell you when you can grow and when you can have an increase on your line of credit.

The banker is a necessity. The banker for your business may come in different forms: friendly investors, traditional local community banker, venture capital investors, private equity, and SBA loans. Whatever the source, there is an unspoken word and, in most cases, a contractual responsibility to diligently and profitably operate the business so that investors, lenders and others can recover their money. If you goof up, goof off, or play too much golf when the business goes down, you go down, the investors get caught holding the bag, and the bankers hold the collateral.

Let's move forward under the idea of the business owner and banker relationship. You will need the banker for a line of credit, for equipment loans, and there may be a few more useful services the bank may perform. Once taking the loan, the disclosed target items must be purchased and placed in service in your business to enhance the profit pursued by you.

When you take a loan and put the money into your business, then over time repay the loan. The banker begins to have confidence in you, and therefore, more loans can become available for your business.

How much a banker will lend is not quantifiable because there are a lot of factors, such as character, confidence, trust, responsible behavior, and many other personal qualities that a banker and the bank loan committee consider.

There is no need to pick on the banker because, at the end of the day, the banker and your banker customer relationship can be a great experience. It is on the back of the business owner to perform and deliver the funds back to the bank on time. This is the best method to get another and bigger loan.

Maintaining a good banking relationship with a commercial bank that can loan money to your business offers numerous benefits. Here are some of the primary purposes, values, and benefits:

**Ease of Access to Capital:** A positive banking relationship can ease the process of securing loans when your business needs them. When the bank is familiar with your business and trusts your ability to repay, they are more likely to approve loan requests, potentially with faster processing times.

**Better Terms and Rates:** Good relationships can lead to favorable interest rates and loan terms, which can save your business significant money over the life of a loan.

**Increased Flexibility:** If your business faces temporary financial hardships, a strong relationship with your bank can provide more flexibility in terms of repayment schedules or restructuring the loan.

**Tailored Financial Products:** Banks often design specific financial products or services for their loyal clients. If they understand your business well, they can offer tailored solutions that best fit your needs.

**Financial Advice:** A good banker can serve as an advisor, helping you navigate complex financial decisions and offering insights into market conditions or opportunities for growth. The banker, on a daily basis, sees a lot of business customers and learns from their experiences.

**Network Opportunities:** Banks often facilitate networking events or introduce clients to potential business partners, customers, or even investors. Bankers know a lot of people who can be helpful to your business's success.

**Credibility:** A strong relationship with a reputable commercial bank can enhance your business's credibility in the eyes of suppliers, customers, and potential partners.

**Ease in Everyday Operations:** Day-to-day operations, like processing payroll, handling payments, and managing cash flows, can become smoother with the support of a bank that understands your business.

**Risk Management:** A good banking relationship can help in managing risks, offering products like hedging against currency fluctuations or advising on cash flow management during uncertain times.

**Business Growth and Development:** With the financial support and advisory services of a bank, businesses can pursue expansion projects, acquire assets, or even pursue mergers and acquisitions more confidently.

**Feedback on Business Health:** Banks routinely assess the creditworthiness and financial health of their business clients. This ongoing scrutiny can provide businesses with feedback and insights into their financial performance, which they can use to make informed decisions.

**Peace of Mind:** Knowing you have a supportive financial partner can provide peace of mind, allowing you to focus more on core business functions. Not only is it worthwhile, it is imperative that you establish a good banking relationship with the manager of your bank branch.

For these reasons and more, it's essential for businesses to cultivate and maintain strong banking relationships. This not only offers immediate financial advantages but also long-term strategic benefits that can be pivotal in a company's growth and success.

The banker, if you keep them informed, may, over time, gain great confidence in you and your business. Then, you may grow to achieve large loan amounts that will allow your business to grow and prosper. It is up to the entrepreneur to groom, culture, and perfect this relationship, usually through excellent performance.

There are no known large businesses that became large without getting a bank loan.

## Cash Flow Statements

Now that you are getting familiar with reports and using them as a navigational map, here for the entrepreneurial owner, it is a must to keep this report in your top desk drawer. This is the cash flow statement. There is software in the marketplace that will produce this report. Your bookkeeper can produce most of it, leaving space for you to fill in the blanks. As chief cash manager, you have to have an idea about the timing of what cash is coming in and what cash needs to go out. The cash flow statement will be your guidance in this regard.

Frequently, you need to view the reports, such as the aged trial balance for accounts receivable. The owner needs to call or have a very sturdy staff member call customers behind on their invoice payments. You, as owner, set the policy about extending credit to customers. Many businesses have shifted to a money upfront policy. Some businesses do a one-third down, one-third when halfway, and one-third when finished with the project.

This way, you are not the bank for the customer, and the flow of cash will be in better timing for when you need to pay money out to keep vendors happy or to receive your vendor's incentive of a 4% discount if paid by the fifth of the month.

The cash flow statement (CFS) is a financial statement that summarizes the movement of cash and cash equivalents that come in and go out of a company. This includes cash from investment sources and crypto receipts. The CFS measures how well a company manages its cash position, meaning how well the company generates cash to pay its debt obligations and fund its operating expenses.

The cash flow statement is a financial statement that provides a collection of data about all cash inflows that a company receives from its ongoing operations and external lending sources. It also includes a prioritized list of all cash outflows that pay for business expenses and loan commitments during a monthly or quarterly period. This data is obtained from the analysis.

As one of the three main financial statements, the cash flow statement complements the balance sheet and the income statement. The flow of cash through the business is like the blood flow through the human body.

There are several kinds of cash flow statements in the marketplace. The cash flow statement that comes with your balance sheet and income statement may be incomprehensible to the business owner. It is better to sit with your chief of accounting and the two of you construct a cash flow statement that is easy to read and easy to follow and has attached schedules that add clarity to the business owner.

Your business may be generating sales, but collections are delayed because of the terms of the contract. On the other hand, expenses to pay landlords, suppliers, payroll, vendors, and utility bills are constant and due on the first day of every month. The cash flow statement is a very important part of operating the business.

This gives you a bird's eye view and ensures you have the necessary cash to face the obligations due on the first day of each month. One business tip is to negotiate your lease and other payment obligations to be due on the 10th day of each month. This gives you a chance from the first through the tenth day to collect from customers and then pay comfortably and timely your obligations on the 10th day of each month.

Most entrepreneurial owners don't have a formal written report, but when they worry, they worry about whether they have enough cash on hand to meet their upcoming expense obligations. Your cash flow statement should be constructed so that your worries become less because you know from the cash flow report that you are on solid ground and able to meet your upcoming financial obligations. The cash flow statement is part of the final exam in my entrepreneurship class.

The cash flow statement will show the timing of when payments come in, and then you can set a date and priority for payments going out. The outbound payments have to be on time to make you look credible to the landlord and key suppliers. Other vendors can receive less priority. Timely payments keep your credit score up. Some vendor payments do not affect your credit score; you will want to know who these vendors are!

Knowing how to balance payments coming in and payments going out is essential to being successful in managing and running a business. Having a policy to set a certain amount in a savings account to take the bumps out of the road is a great idea. Many business owners report this makes them feel more comfortable.

So now is the time to review the utility of the Balance Sheet and the Income Statement.

The Balance Sheet: An accounting professor gave me the best short answer to what the balance sheet is. The balance sheet is a list of the business ownership and equity. It contains the things that the business owns. The balance sheet is a photo "snapshot" at midnight, on the last day of the month, of the financial ownership position of the business.

There is a math formula behind the creation of the balance sheet.

Assets minus liabilities equals the owner's equity

$$\frac{\begin{array}{r}A\\-L\end{array}}{\mathbf{OE}}$$

The list of assets is prepared in accordance with Generally Accepted Accounting Principles. The assets are listed at the original cost, not at the appreciated market value. You make a solid list of the assets of the business following a very traditional style of categorization.

Next in the balance sheet are listed the liabilities and the debts of the business. These obligations are also listed in a very well-established traditional style.

When the assets are subtracted from the liabilities, mathematically, you arrive at what is left over. This leftover amount is considered to be the "equity" the shareholders have in the company. The balance sheet is a very important document for the owner to know about and the banker to analyze to determine if you qualify for a new loan.

Here is the more technical explaination of the balance sheet. A balance sheet is a financial statement that provides a snapshot of a company's financial position at a specific point in time, typically the end of a specific period. It consists of two main sections: assets and liabilities, both of which must balance. Assets represent what a company owns, including cash, investments, and property. Liabilities encompass what a company owes, such as debts and obligations. The third component is shareholders' equity, representing the residual interest in the company's assets after deducting liabilities. The balance sheet reflects the company's financial health and is a crucial tool, for analytical purposes, for investors, creditors, and management.

The Income Statement: Statement of Income, aka, Profit and Loss Report; these terms are used in entrepreneurial conversations to describe the sales of the business for the measured period and then identically match the sales to the cost of making those sales; the raw materials and labor used to create the goods or services sold during this measured period. So, you get the idea you first accurately list the sales for the period, then subtract from those sales the exact costs of making those sales.

The Sales, less the costs of goods sold, equal the gross profit

$$\begin{array}{r} S \\ - CGS \\ \hline \mathbf{GP} \end{array}$$

The gross profit number, when measured correctly, is what you have to constantly watch as the owner of the business. Are you ahead of or behind the targeted number that you were hoping for? Most business owners track gross profit by looking at the percentage of the gross profit and comparing this to sales, and then you get a percentage of, let's say, 55%.

Then, there are more costs of business operations that must be considered. The administrative expenses, the overhead expenses, and the allocation for depreciation during the measured period.

The Gross Profit, less the general and administrative expenses, including depreciation, will yield the net profit

$$\begin{array}{r} GP \\ -GA \\ \hline \mathbf{NP} \end{array}$$

The net profit of the business is what professional company managers are measured by. Most professional CEOs call the net profit the earnings for the measured period. The CEO's life depends on what the earnings of the company are for each quarterly period.

The statement of income, often referred to as the income statement or profit and loss statement (P&L), is a crucial financial document that provides a detailed summary of a company's revenues, expenses, gains, and losses over a specific period of time, typically a fiscal quarter or year. It serves as one of the three primary financial statements, along with the balance sheet and cash flow statement, and is essential for assessing a business's financial performance and profitability. Here's a technical breakdown of the statement of income and its significance to advanced business owners:

## Components of the Statement of Income:

Revenues (Sales or Sales Revenue): This is the top line of the income statement and represents the total income generated by the company through its primary operations. It includes sales of goods or services, royalties, and any other forms of income directly related to the core business activities.

Cost of Goods Sold (COGS): COGS represents the direct costs associated with producing the goods or services sold during the period. This includes raw materials, labor, and manufacturing expenses.

Gross Profit: Gross profit is calculated by subtracting COGS from revenues. It indicates how much money the company retains after covering the costs directly associated with its products or services sold during the period.

**Operating Expenses:** These are the indirect costs incurred to run the business day-to-day. They include items such as salaries, rent, utilities, marketing expenses, and depreciation.

**Operating Income (Operating Profit):** Operating income is calculated by subtracting operating expenses from gross profit. It reflects the profitability of a company's core operations before considering interest and taxes.

**Other Income and Expenses:** This section accounts for any non-operating income or expenses, such as interest income, interest expenses, gains or losses from investments, and other non-core business activities.

**Net Income (Net Profit or Net Loss):** Net income is the bottom line of the income statement and represents the company's overall profitability after accounting for all expenses and income, including taxes. A positive net income indicates a profit, while a negative net income indicates a loss.

## Significance to Advanced Business Owners:

**Performance Assessment:** The income statement helps advanced business owners assess the company's financial performance over a specific period. It provides a clear picture of whether the business is generating profits or incurring losses.

**Decision Making:** Business owners can use the income statement to make informed decisions regarding pricing, cost control, and investment strategies. It helps identify areas where cost reductions or revenue increases may be needed.

**Investor and Lender Relations:** Investors and lenders often rely on the income statement to evaluate a company's financial health and creditworthiness. A strong and consistent positive net income can attract investors and secure loans at favorable terms.

**Tax Planning:** Understanding the components of the income statement is crucial for tax planning. Business owners can optimize their tax strategies based on knowing their income and expenses.

**Benchmarking:** Business owners can compare their income statements with industry peers to gauge their competitiveness and identify areas for improvement.

**Strategic Planning:** The income statement is a valuable tool for long-term strategic planning. It helps business owners set realistic financial goals and track progress toward achieving them.

The statement of income is a critical financial document that provides a comprehensive view of a company's financial performance. Advanced business owners use it to make strategic decisions, to gain insight as to what needs to be improved within business operations, attract investors and lenders, and assess the overall health and profitability of their enterprises.

When bankers are not interested, start-up businesses turn to venture capital firms. Venture capital firms have experienced investors who will advance you money in exchange for a percentage ownership in your company.

If you want to start out owning less than 100% of your company, then venture capital is available to those who make a compelling pitch to the venture capitalists. Sometimes, venture capital firms will promise to participate in advancing the product in the marketplace. They could help you with your marketing and product placement steps. When this happens, giving up a percentage of ownership in the company is not as painful.

If you own 100%, you might, through your talents, grow the company to $10 million in sales. With the venture capital, you will own 80% of a company that does $350 million in sales. Life is about choices; you have to choose which one you desire to have.

Securing venture capital funding for a start-up is a competitive process, and there are several steps you can take to increase your chances of obtaining venture capital. Here are some key strategies to consider.

Develop a solid business plan. Craft a comprehensive and well researched business plan that clearly outlines your start-up's vision, market opportunity, competitive advantage, financial projections, and growth strategy. Show how your business will generate substantial returns for potential investors.

Build a strong team. Investors are often interested in the people behind the start-up. Assemble a team with relevant expertise and a track record of success in your industry. A strong team demonstrates your ability to execute the business plan effectively.

Create a compelling pitch deck. Prepare a concise and visually appealing pitch deck that highlights the key aspects of your business. Include information on the problem you're solving, your unique value proposition, market size, revenue model, and go-to-market strategy. Be persuasive and focus on the potential for high growth and returns.

Network and seek introductions. Leverage your network to connect with potential venture capital firms and individual investors. Attend industry events, join start-up communities, and seek introductions through mutual connections. Building relationships and gaining warm introductions can significantly increase your chances of getting noticed by investors.

Research and target the right investors. Conduct thorough research to identify venture capital firms or individual investors who have a track record of investing in your industry or similar start-ups. Tailor your pitch to align with their investment preferences and philosophies. A targeted approach increases the likelihood of finding investors interested in your business.

Demonstrate traction and milestones. If possible, show early signs of market traction or customer adoption. Highlight key milestones achieved, such as partnerships, user growth, revenue, or product development progress and patents obtained. Tangible evidence of progress indicates your start-up's potential for success and reduces the perceived risks for investors. You will want to properly explain the competition and reveal if you have any patent rights on your product.

Be prepared for due diligence. Anticipate that investors will conduct due diligence to assess the viability and potential risks of your business. Prepare by organizing your financial records, legal documents, intellectual property rights, and any relevant industry or market research. Being well prepared demonstrates professionalism and instills confidence in investors.

Consider professional assistance. If you're new to fundraising or need additional expertise, consider seeking help from professionals such as start-up consultants or experienced advisors who specialize in venture capital financing. They can guide you through the process, offer valuable insights, and help improve your chances of securing funding.

Remember that venture capital funding is highly competitive, and success is never guaranteed. It often requires persistence, resilience, and a willingness to learn from feedback and adapt your approach. Keep refining your pitch and strategy based on investor interactions and market dynamics, and don't be discouraged by setbacks.

**CHAPTER 5**

# Self-Awareness and Self-Help

Who are you? What do you want from life? Are you looking for a safe and easy way out? Are you looking to collect the greatest number of pensions at age 65? Are you looking to accomplish something? Do you want to feel proud about what you have built? Do you want to pass on a legacy to your family, friends, relatives, and charities?

Self-awareness will help you choose a career path. Your drive and determination will help make you suited for owning your own business.

Is what you are doing today leading you onto the path that you want to be on tomorrow? Education is one of the leading components that will help you succeed in owning your own business.

For you, a career path is a list of steps to take in your life, to progress into different or more advanced roles at work. Traditionally, this means a raise in pay. Many people want a raise in pay, but they do nothing to learn more about anything, and thus, they may stay a long time in the same job with no advancement.

To get ahead, you have to do something, want something, and then take some initiative to get what you want.

Your career path is a series of jobs and experiences that help employees reach their ultimate career objectives and future goals. This career path, from the dedicated employee mindset, will do something to lead to a reason the company will advance the person.

Career pathing is the practice of planning an employee's future career opportunities within an organization. Learning about career pathing can help you improve employee output and retention rates if you work in a company's HR or management department. The HR department often needs to lean less on compliance and more on employee needs and assistance in helping make strides and steps to advance on the company's organizational chart.

The self-employed person will break out of the pack as an employee and start a business that will provide a feeling of accomplishment and allow you the freedom to choose when you go to work and when you go home from work. If you are self-employed, you are allowed to go where you want and when you want. Self-employment provides a situation where there is no one to ask when you want to go to the beach, play golf or tennis, or just lay in the sun and collect vitamin D.

You are the one to pick and choose. If you choose something as an employee or self-employed person, put your 100% into what you are doing. So many people I talk to about career paths look at their assigned job and the job steps, then try to take shortcuts by doing only half of the steps, then standing back and expecting to win the Employee of the Month award.

The high achievers in this world look at their job tasks, and they do 200% of what is required and then take their own personal time to do outside research to learn how to do their job better. Sometimes, they learn by learning more about and examining what their competitors are doing. Other times, it is just research to learn more about their assigned task so that they can do it better.

To determine whether you are fit for self-employment, you have to know that your belief system and your long list of fears and doubts are holding you back. This is combined with the fact that all steps of self-employment are new and different to you; you have not done this before.

Our belief system refers to the collection of beliefs, values, and principles that shape an individual's perception of the world and guide their decisions and behaviors. Many of these beliefs are gathered overtime and date back to early childhood.

Our belief system encompasses religious, cultural, philosophical, employment, and personal convictions, influencing how we interpret events, interact with others, and pursue goals. Our belief system can be flexible or rigid, open minded or closed off, and greatly impacts our worldview, resilience, and capacity for personal growth.

If we are rigid in our beliefs, we may not be up for a new adventure. If we are open to learning more and have a give-it-a-try outlook, or have a I-want-to-do-it-myself outlook, we have a better chance for success in self-employment.

Many people hold back from self-employment because they have certain fears and beliefs holding them back. They have a fear of failure. They possess a belief that they are not worthy of being the owner of a business. They have a fear of the unknown and fear about things they have never done before.

To become self-employed, you have to know yourself, trust yourself, believe in yourself, and be able to take a look at who you are and where you would like to be.

In entering self-employment, you have to have a sketch in your mind or better on paper of what you would do and how this could be competitive in the marketplace. You have to look at your core values. What are your core values? Do you feel ambitious? What type of business do you envision owning? What type of profession do you envision participating as a principal in? Do you want a yoga studio, dance studio, ceramic do-it-yourself store, construction company, paint-with-wine studio, manufacturing, food processing, software or app development, or do you want to own a franchise?

There are plenty of people who are good doctors, but very few of them actually become owners of their own businesses. Many doctors wake up to the idea when they understand and discover that their income tax rate will go from 35% of their salary down to around 10% of their salary.

They will be able to purchase their office building rather than pay a landlord's rent. When they finish being a doctor, they have enjoyed years of low-income tax costs, they have millions of dollars saved in their pension plan, and they have free and clear ownership of their home and office building, which over the years have appreciated in value. Many doctors are more ambitious and become experts in residential and commercial rental properties, and then at retirement age, they have a huge net worth and they easily have the ability to retire in comfort.

The point is you don't have to be a doctor to achieve these things in life. I have seen many in the manufacturing industry, realtors, farming industry, construction industry, and winery business, and they learn how to structure their businesses, invest their earnings, fund their retirement accounts, and build their financial net worth. It is a process that you, too, can learn to do.

There is an old saying there is no one business that will make you rich. In every industry, there is a good business person that ends their career rich, with bags of money, because they have built their net worth and earned the ability to retire in any city in the country with style and comfort.

To continue with your self-assessment, you have to examine and ask yourself? What do you do better than anyone else? What is your passion and pleasure? What is your unique skill or craft?

What will be your company's niche? Do you want to retire in comfort and style and enjoy happiness? What will be your proposed business marketing strategy? Who is your target customer, and are there enough of these customers in your geographic market area? Realistically, look at your beliefs and the limitations holding you back from joining the ranks of the self-employed.

Oftentimes, it's the high achievers that are the ones best suited for self-employment. Those who desire safety, no bumps, and do not want to work too hard should remain employees.

From my observations there is an interesting phenomenon in the marketplace. If you are born, raised and live in the country there are no employers there to generously give you a job. If there are, there are very few. Thus, people who are age 25 to 55 have a high likelihood of becoming self-employed.

If you are born, raised and live in the city and your parents worked as employees of a company, agency or institution you too may initially be drawn to get a job as an employee for a company. So, consider these factors when you begin to design what type of self-employment activity you want to become engaged in.

## Self-Help Industry

When the self-help industry was discovered, it was not self-help for accountants or engineers. It was self-help for the marketing people to give them poise, confidence, and the belief that they could make the next cold call and close the sale using well-known techniques.

The early stages of the self-improvement industry had such luminaries as Dale Carnegie, who might be considered the "father of self-improvement."

Dale was an American writer, lecturer, and developer of courses in self-improvement, salesmanship, corporate training, public speaking, and interpersonal skills.

There are some that can be traced in history back to ancient Egyptian times when a form of self-help was present. But in the 1980's self-help started to bloom in America. The self-help industry is a multi-billion-dollar industry that provides products and services to help people improve their lives, their jobs, and their businesses.

The self-help industry provides a variety of services, such as life coaching, motivational speaking, books, tapes, CD seminars, workshops, and online, on demand courses. These self-improvement courses will alert you to your belief system and how to change your beliefs so that you can feel that you, too, can succeed in self-employment.

The self-help industry has many colorful characters. I remember when attending the National Speakers Association meetings, you could approach and shake hands with these people, and they usually would share a little nugget of knowledge.

The industry got quite a push when Tony Robbins began to roll. He had some background in the self-help industry as the frontman for other speakers. Then he put one giant foot forward and began on his own. Then came some cassette tapes touted by the famous NFL quarterback Fran Tarkenton. Fran then told you why you should buy these tapes.

Tony set records with his own version of seminars, where you could attend the basic seminar and then be upsold on the next seminar with a fire walk in between. Tony Robbins is an American author, coach, speaker, and philanthropist. He is known for his infomercials, seminars, and self-help books, including the books "Unlimited Power" and "Awaken the Giant Within."

Some think these self-help books are the secret to unlocking personal wellness, inner peace, or financial stability. These books will make you feel more confident, solve your relationship woes, and lead to a life of abundance, wealth, and prosperity.

Brian Tracy cannot be left out of the mix. Brian produced books and cassette tapes that took over the sales training programs for many large companies.

Besides being a personal friend, Brian Tracy is a Canadian born American champion motivational public speaker and self-development author. He is the author of over eighty books that have been translated into dozens of languages. His popular books are "Earn What You're Really Worth," and "Psychology of Achievement."

Brian made hundreds of contributions to making people perform better. One of his themes was, "There are no limits on what you can achieve with your life, except the limits you accept in your mind." "Move out of your comfort zone. You can only grow if you are willing to feel awkward and uncomfortable when you try something new."

There were many other luminaries and well-known public speakers in the early days of self-help development.

Then, the self-help industry expanded into other areas and topics: change management, how to feel better, how to overcome your fears, execution with precision, and striving for excellence. The meatier topics have been: confidence building, career development, motivation (light the fire), communication topics, self-understanding, leadership, optimism positivity, organization and prioritize, time management, business relationships, love relationships, productivity purpose, passion, vision (discover yours), the assertiveness attitude.

These were all courses, books, and seminars to help you succeed in business after you had completed your formal education. To succeed in business, you must continue with self-directed education that will help you discover the next step to take to grow and expand your business.

Ok, I understand the last thing one wants to do once they have completed 4 to 6 years of college study is to hear that you have to take more classes.

Well, you should take a break and reflect; then, if you decide that you want to succeed, you should take some courses that will help you sing songs to the customers so that they flock to your doors, take leadership class so you will learn the principles of C-Suite management and how to create a vision of the future.

Then, look at yourself and your personality. What do you need to put a little frosting on the cake so that you understand your business better, feel better, and are aligned to succeed in your chosen field, endeavor, or business start-up?

Take classes that will help you improve. Maybe if you improve your public speaking skills, you will be asked to present to rooms of 1000 or more the whole time, reminding the people about your product or service to attract more business to your door.

Maybe you are the featured speaker at your industry convention, where everyone there, including bankers and vendors, walks away knowing more about your business. Then, over time, you can become the Harvey McKay (Swim with the Sharks) of your industry, where your name becomes a household word, and your business flourishes because of it.

Self-study, self-directed learning, and more classes in the right direction will help you move from a small business to a medium-sized business with less stress and more enthusiasm with more people on your side. Below is a walk through of what self-help can do for you.

## Introduction:

In the fast paced world of entrepreneurship, success often hinges on an individual's ability to learn, adapt, and grow continuously. While innate skills, ambition, and a strategic mindset are undoubtedly essential, the importance of personal development cannot be overstated. Let's explore the invaluable value that high quality self-help classes bring to entrepreneurs, enabling them to unlock their true potential and thrive in today's competitive business landscape.

## Enhancing Self-Awareness:

One of the fundamental pillars of success for any entrepreneur lies in self-awareness. Understanding one's strengths, weaknesses, and unique qualities is crucial when making critical business decisions. High quality self-help classes offer entrepreneurs a profound opportunity to embark on a journey of self-discovery. By engaging in introspective exercises, goal setting techniques, and practical strategies, entrepreneurs can better understand themselves and their aspirations, allowing them to align their actions with their true purpose.

## Building Resilience and Emotional Intelligence:

Entrepreneurship is a rollercoaster ride filled with ups and downs, challenges, and setbacks. To navigate this demanding journey, entrepreneurs must cultivate resilience and emotional intelligence. Self-help classes provide invaluable tools and frameworks to strengthen one's mental and emotional fortitude. Through expert guidance, entrepreneurs can develop coping mechanisms, effective stress and anger management techniques, and enhanced interpersonal skills, enabling them to handle adversity with poise and grace, recover from failures, and foster healthy relationships within their professional and personal lives.

## Sharpening Leadership Skills:

Entrepreneurs are the driving force behind their ventures, and effective leadership is crucial for long-term success. Self-help classes tailored specifically for entrepreneurs offer comprehensive leadership development programs, honing essential skills such as communication, decision making, strategic planning, and team management. By leveraging proven methodologies, entrepreneurs can acquire the knowledge and insights necessary to inspire their teams, foster a positive work culture, and make confident, informed decisions that drive their businesses forward.

## Fostering Continuous Learning and Growth Mindset:

The business landscape is constantly evolving, and entrepreneurs must stay ahead of the curve to seize emerging opportunities. High-quality self-help classes act as a catalyst for continuous learning, encouraging entrepreneurs to adopt a growth mindset. These classes provide entrepreneurs with a competitive edge by exposing them to the latest industry trends, innovation methodologies, and best practices. Moreover, they foster a culture of lifelong learning, empowering entrepreneurs to embrace change, adapt to new technologies, and consistently evolve their skills and knowledge.

## Expanding Professional Networks:

Successful entrepreneurs recognize the power of networking and the opportunities it brings. Self-help classes not only provide a platform for learning but also facilitate meaningful connections with like-minded individuals. These classes bring together a diverse group of entrepreneurs, offering a fertile ground for collaboration, partnerships, and knowledge sharing. By engaging in group discussions, workshops, and networking events, entrepreneurs can expand their professional networks, gain fresh perspectives, and find potential mentors or investors who can play a pivotal role in their entrepreneurial journey.

In the dynamic world of entrepreneurship, investing in personal growth and development is a strategic choice that can significantly impact an entrepreneur's journey toward success. High quality self-help classes empower entrepreneurs with self-awareness, resilience, leadership skills, and a growth mindset, which can unlock doors and opportunities. By finally unlocking their full potential, entrepreneurs can navigate challenges, seize opportunities, and drive their ventures towards sustainable growth and meet success. As the old adage goes, "Invest in yourself, and your business will thrive."

## Time Management

In talking about self-help, let's discuss time management. As an entrepreneur, especially an entrepreneur driving a growth company, how well you utilize your time is very important.

Time management has many dimensions; it is not one directional. How we pick and choose what we do and then choose not to delegate the task begins to paint how efficient we are as executives. Delegation, training of others, and focus on the target are very important parts of time management.

Time management is an important skill pivotal to personal and professional success. Effectively utilizing time allows individuals to accomplish their goals, maintain productivity, and minimize stress. It involves making conscious choices about how to allocate one's time, setting priorities, and efficiently completing tasks.

Time management encompasses various dimensions. The first dimension is planning. It involves setting clear objectives, breaking them down into smaller tasks, and creating a roadmap to achieve them. Planning enables individuals to stay focused, avoid distractions, and make the most of their time.

Another dimension is prioritization, set priorities. Effective time managers identify the most important tasks that require immediate attention. They distinguish between urgent and non-urgent tasks, allowing them to allocate their time and resources accordingly.

Delegation is another crucial aspect of time management. Recognizing that they cannot do everything themselves, effective time managers delegate tasks to others with the necessary skills and resources. Delegation not only frees up time for the manager to focus on high-priority tasks but also promotes teamwork and empowers team members to develop and improve their skills.

As the captain of the ship, it is vital to drive the company with a clear focus on the target. A captain sets the vision, aligns the team, and ensures that everyone is working towards a common goal. Time management is essential in this role as it enables the captain to prioritize tasks, allocate resources efficiently, and make informed decisions to steer the company in the right direction.

Time management involves planning, prioritization, and delegation. It is a multi-dimensional skill that helps individuals make the most of their time, achieve their goals, and maintain a balanced and fulfilling life. Effective time management is even more critical, as it enables leaders to guide their teams toward success by staying focused on the target.

## Amassing Wealth with Comfort and Determination

Another topic worthy of mention is the idea of amassing wealth. Many people are not comfortable with this idea, and, as a consequence, many things booby trap themselves from getting to the place of amassing great wealth.

Overcoming the fear of amassing great wealth is a personal journey that may vary for each individual. However, here are some general suggestions that may help:

**Reflect on your values:** Take some time to consider your personal values and beliefs about wealth. Understand what wealth means to you and how it aligns with your overall life goals. This self-reflection can help you develop a healthy mindset towards wealth accumulation.

**Educate yourself:** Learn about the responsibilities and opportunities that come with wealth. Understanding how wealth can be used to make a positive impact in various areas of life, such as philanthropy, investing in sustainable ventures, or supporting social causes, can help alleviate any guilt or fear associated with wealth accumulation. When accumulating wealth, the act of accumulation should be the first priority, accumulation and preservation. When some people gain wealth, they feel guilty, which may cause them to give away their grandchildren's inheritance.

**Seek professional advice:** Consult with financial advisors with many high-net-worth clients, as they can help you navigate the complexities of managing wealth. Seek advice that will help adjust your mindset that having and accumulating wealth is okay for you. Financial advisors can assist in creating a comprehensive financial plan that aligns with your goals and tolerance for risk, which helps you make informed decisions and mitigates any fears or concerns you may have. Financial planning has to be interwoven with your estate planning steps.

**Surround yourself with like-minded individuals:** Engage with a community of individuals who share similar values and beliefs about wealth. This can provide a supportive environment where you can openly discuss your concerns, gain insights from others, and find reassurance that you are not alone in your journey. When people share information, you may learn something that will make your portfolio stronger and your mental outlook more calm and more comfortable with the wealth that you have accumulated.

**Give back to society:** Once you have really amassed wealth and feel comfortable not acting out of guilt, you may find contentment in giving back. Pay it forward! Consider using your wealth to make a positive impact on the world. Philanthropy or engaging in charitable activities can provide a sense of purpose and fulfilment.

**Practice gratitude:** After working hard to create a mindset of wealth accumulation. Then, cultivate a mindset of gratitude for the opportunities and resources that wealth provides. Regularly acknowledge and appreciate the privileges and advantages that come with your wealth. Gratitude can help shift the focus from fear to appreciation and create a healthier relationship with your wealth.

Remember, overcoming fear is a personal process that may take time. Working with professionals, seeking support from your network, and engaging in ongoing self-reflection to develop a positive and balanced perspective on wealth accumulation can be beneficial. Several psychologists across the country will help you gain a mindset that accumulating wealth is okay.

In speaking with psychologists, this was their take on this issue of timidness or fear of accumulating wealth.

There could be several psychological reasons why executives of privately held companies may fear accumulating personal wealth. They may feel guilty about amassing wealth while their employees struggle financially.

Fear of judgment or backlash from society or their peers may make them apprehensive about displaying their wealth. They might also fear the potential loss of personal relationships or the feeling of being disconnected from others if they become too affluent.

Largely, some individuals may have an underlying fear of the responsibilities and pressures that come with wealth, such as managing investments or dealing with increased public scrutiny. A desire to maintain a sense of humility and focus on the company's success rather than personal gain could also contribute to their reluctance to accumulate personal wealth.

The wealth accumulation mindset is something to work on. There is also the person who came from humble beginnings now has a chance to accumulate wealth, but instead of accumulation, they spend and spend and spend until they are deep in debt.

They like the feeling of doing well and having wealth, but they have not adopted a method of accumulating; instead, they get involved with lavish parties, an entourage of people to accompany them, and wildly spend money with and on friends. Both of these prospects and a few more need to be visited by a healthcare professional. This way, you can have a healthy outlook about doing well, enjoying success, and accumulating and growing your financial net worth.

CHAPTER 6

# Entrepreneurial Operations: DO SOMETHING!

It's all about choice!

The first thing that you need to do is throw a dart at the board and choose what you would like to do. What self-employed business would you choose to do? Where is your passion? What self-employment endeavor will require you to go to the golf course and meet with potential customers, win their hearts, and make them your customers?

Where is your passion, where is your skill set, what do you like to do, what is the market missing? This is the search that you must do. More importantly, what you must do is take a stand and choose something.

Many people freeze at this point and rationalize that staying at the 8-5 job is much easier than committing and taking a stand and then "doing something." Well, at an early age, it is a good time to "do something." Do this for your family and create a legacy. Leave something for your children and grandchildren to do. Break out of the pack, get away from 8-5, own your own business, and gain your freedom, independence, and the chance to make three times as much money and pay two-thirds less income tax than the boring 8-5 job.

I have known people who want to do something, and it is on their mind, it is on the back burner, then what happens is they turn 100 years old, or they have 100 excuses why they cannot choose one business opportunity and get started. The top excuses are fear and the lack of belief in themselves. A large group of people have never done this before; therefore, they are not going to give it a try.

It can be simple: if you want to share your recipe with the world about your wonderful chili beans, you don't need to have $100 million to start a factory and purchase equipment. The quick of foot would find a co-packer who would make the product and put it into a sealed can. Then left for you is the branding and marketing function. You have to have a brand for the product that will say, "Trust this product," "It is delicious," and "Made with high quality ingredients."

Then you have to get the product in front of people. Light a fire under all restaurants that serve chili beans but don't have the time or equipment to make their own chili. This aligns with the entrepreneurial principle of why sell it by the 8oz can when I can sell by the 1-gallon can. Restaurants will buy a commercial quantity in a large can.

Then, take it to the people and hand out free samples in the church parking lot. Find trade shows with consumers who are likely to enjoy your product. Go to the county fair in every county of every state and sell the product and hand out samples, then explain the product using the megaphone to the crowd. Create some reason to buy the product and take this coupon home for reorders!

When you catch that entrepreneurial spirit, you will think of, imagine, and create ways to get your product in front of people who would enjoy your product, consume your product, and then come back and buy more of your product. Get involved and do something so you, too, can catch the "entrepreneurial spirit."

Where there is a will within you, there is a way for you to get product recognition. Once the product is recognized, it will "sell through" the grocery stores and, ultimately, the larger big box stores like Costco.

Once you have retail and specialty food store "sell through," you have properly launched your product, and then your focus re-joins how you make the product and product improvement.

Then comes the time to introduce new products in your product line, increase the retailers who carry your brand. Monitor that you are getting "sell through" in the retail stores. Over time and with the success of higher sales, you will find several acres of land and build a factory to produce your expanding line of products.

Counseling entrepreneurs is where I spend a lot of my time, giving them confidence, reducing their fears, getting their spouse on board, and then taking the chance. We provide the guard rails so that things go straight down the road, not a start that goes off road and out into the weeds. Many times, the young entrepreneur has not done this before and gets lost and ends up off the road. Remember to stay on the road. There have been a thousand people before with similar products starting out, and there is a specific path to follow but many ways to travel down the road.

What happens when you start a business unprepared?

Most businesses are started by people with good skills at their product or service who haven't acquired the basic skills or knowledge about business or they still assume that business acumen is a minor part of the new business equation.

The classic example is when a good mechanic starts their own repair shop. This is the technician who does a very good job of repairing the car, but they also have to come to an understanding that business knowledge and business skills are a very important part of succeeding in business. There is more to it than fixing the engine.

You need to have a valid legal contract for the customer to sign. You need to have a complete accounting and list of what parts went into the job and how many hours of labor went into the job. You have to establish a labor shop rate that considers the employees' wages and the overhead for the business.

All of this is needed to be able to present a bill and collect money for that bill before the car leaves the lot. Then, you need a system to get the money into the bank. At the end of the month, you need cash reserves to pay your landlord and suppliers.

There is a large list of surrounding events that you have to be able to do to actually run the business. It's the same for the good dentist who can fix teeth but knows nothing about administrative chores, payroll requirements, scheduling, marketing, and other business obligations.

To begin to understand how to run the business side of the business, one has to study a fully developed company and then know one day you too will need all these separate departments.

For now, you need to know that you will have to wear all ten hats of the entrepreneur. Later, you can develop your HR department, but for now, you need a chapter and verse of an employee handbook that sets forth all of your business's rules, policies, tolerances, and boundaries.

Without an employee handbook, you are just bait for an employee-oriented law firm that loves to sue employers for overtime pay, lack of paid holidays, and, by the way, the two weeks of vacation pay for the employee who worked for you for seven months.

One will soon learn that running a business is done by many sets of systems and procedures, all leading to the next step. With the proper set of systems and procedures in place, the business runs smoothly. The customers come in, they are well served, they leave their car, the employee does the mechanical steps of repairing the car, the owner checks the work and test drives the car, the customer is called, and the customer comes back and pays the invoice. Money goes to the bank, and because of good management, there is enough money to pay the vendors, the employees, the rent and the payroll taxes, with enough left over for the owner to take home a salary.

So, analyzing the steps and installing well known business systems and procedures will help the business to continue to run smoothly, month after month, so the owner can take home a bonus at the end of the year.

The aforementioned systems and procedures are not taught in any school, high school, community college, or university, including Harvard and Wharton. These steps and procedures and the underlying supporting steps and procedures are the heart of running a business and our education system does not address them.

I personally have tried introducing financial literacy courses to high schools and community colleges. Something as simple as writing a check, applying for a credit card, discipline to pay back the credit card company, schools dance around the topic.

Then, I did a pitch to public high schools about teaching a money and marriage course addressing money management and adult relationships... The schools would have nothing to do with this because all their systems and procedures are about keeping the students apart, away from each other; they don't want to teach a course on relationships!

This is the thinking of the administrators of our schools. Finally, there are trade schools where you can go to learn how to become a mechanic and repair an engine, but still, no schools teach one how to run an automotive repair shop business, dental office, or law firm.

One has to focus on the surrounding business events that have to occur correctly, on time, and in the proper order. As the owner, you need to set rules and boundaries for your customers to adhere to and comply with.

With your talents, resources, and things you have learned, you will have to learn how to wear or hire these four hats. Accounting, marketing, production manager, and leader. These four disciplines need to be in the mechanic's repair shop, the dentist's office, the construction company, the software developer, or whatever business you operate.

These four core disciplines are necessary to successfully operate a small or medium-sized business. There are other duties and tasks, but these four disciplines must be present and must be polished.

When you own a business and master the business operational steps, it provides much joy and pride of ownership. You feel great each day that something that you created is alive, functioning, and competing in the marketplace. The name of the company is a brand that you are proud of because you stand behind that name, making sure that the product or service is solid, without flaw and is something that will help others.

When you focus on the details, learn the business steps and the functional areas of business, and put them to use when designing your company's systems and procedures, your end result will be a success. Success is something to strive for and accomplish to further your pride of ownership.

Business requires learning, learning something new, learning something that you have not done before. This is a requirement of business to grow and learn then learn from others. If you fail to do this, you have increased the odds of your business's inevitable failure.

Oddly enough, banks have a vested interest in seeing that you learn the proper business steps to run your business, because your survival will heighten the chances of the bank becoming repaid, on outstanding loans.

This is something that private equity firms have learned over the years. Private equity firms will require that you hire competent management consultants to help you install systems and procedures known to work in your industry. Typically, management consulting firms are accounting firms on steroids.

Management consulting firms are not accounting firms interested in issuing your year end audited financial statements. Management consulting firms are business advisors schooled in systems and procedures and organizational structure.

These people know the path and how to install systems and procedures custom tailored to your business enterprise. They know the whole operational aspect of your business and the necessary computers and software and apps to make the business run properly. They know this because this is their business; they have done this one hundred times before for other companies in various stages of development.

These consultants put up the guard rails to see that you stay within the boundaries of reason when operating your company. While the Private Equity firm has a vested interest not only in your survival but also in the height of your earnings. There are lessons to be learned about this.

The idea is for the business owner to find enough information and learn enough subjects to ensure the success of the business.

I once led a group of four: a banker, an attorney, an insurance agent, and an accountant. We taught a class to new and soon-to-be business owners. Each professional laid out for the audience what, from their professional perspective, it takes for a business to succeed. The focus was the same: how to succeed in business. The information was very different from each professional's perspective.

The attorney wanted you to be properly fitted with the proper business entity. C-Corporation, S-Corporation, Partnership, LLC, and the attorney explained the hazards of being a sole proprietor. Then, the attorney was all about contract agreements and ways to seal yourself off from a sour customer or vendor damaging your business through a lawsuit. The attorney stuck to operations and did not cover much labor law, which today could easily be an eight-hour seminar in itself. The attorney went on to explain the need to coordinate your financial planning with your tax planning and your succession planning with your estate planning. The attorney also explained the power you have in designing well your living trust.

The banker explained that soon after starting a business, you will need a loan. Equipment loan, financing for orders received, or a simple business line of credit. The emphasis was that every business should have a way to quickly get equipment loans when needed, and every business should have a line of credit available just in case something by surprise were to come up in the course of doing business.

The banker explained that you, the owner, needed to have credibility; you needed to be credit worthy. The audience quickly noted that they needed to do banking with a bank that was able to issue loans to a business. A bank to help when help was needed. The signal here was to cozy up to a banker, make them your friend, and make them aware of your business and your interest in calling upon them in time of need.

The banker also explained that your business has to show that it has the capacity to take on a loan and then make timely repayments of this loan. A banker looks at your credit history, how you dealt with your loans in the past, and how many times you made late payments.

Credit history, credit reports, and credit score all play a part in your ability to get a loan and the bank's ability to give you a loan. If you present through your credit performance history that you are a credit risk, then the bank cannot give you a loan. The bank could also look at your collateral. Do you have anything of value to the bank that you can pledge to the bank that would make them feel more secure that you will make timely repayments of the loan? Your creditworthiness is an important part of your business to protect.

People have found that if you apply for and get three credit cards, then charge something on them each month. Then, three days before the due date, pay the balance in full. This may boost your credit score into the 800s.

The insurance agent pointed out from the agent's experience the perils that you might encounter and ways to insure against those perils so that the insurance company would pay the bill and you, as the business owner, would not have to pay.

The understanding is that every business owner needs to look at general liability insurance, worker's compensation insurance, office or shop insurance, vehicle insurance for one's self, and know if an employee is driving any vehicle for the business purpose.

Building, office, and home insurance with the proper personal umbrella policy. By the way, there is always life insurance. Insurance is a vital part of your business and can be a part of your pension plan, retirement plan, or estate planning.

You also can look at various kinds of insurance that will overlap with your other insurance that will cover perils that fall through the cracks. You will not want this economic charge to hit your checkbook, so you need to have adequate insurance and umbrella coverage to seal off your exposure to economic damage.

Then, the accountant, the star of the show, would present the need to pay attention to the tax law from the perspective of income tax, social security tax, and payroll tax. Be aware of the IRS as to what it does and what it is supposed to do.

The IRS is the enforcement division of the United States Treasury. Congress passes a tax law, and the IRS makes sure that you pay attention and pay your taxes on time.

Record keeping and record retention are important because for you to pass inspection, in the event of an IRS audit, you have to present a canceled check or equivalent and an invoice to support the deductions that you plan to take in your tax return.

Your ultimate income tax expense can be large if you do not pay attention and can be rather small if you follow all the rules, keep the proper documentation and records, and then participate in tax planning steps to minimize your income tax exposure.

Having books and records is important because, from these records, financial reports can be drafted. If you have sloppy books and records, it would be difficult to prepare the proper reports accurately. Again, the bank has a vested interest in you presenting proper and accurate financial statements at the end of each required reporting period.

With the primary reports, the Balance Sheet, the Profit and Loss Statement, and the Cash Flow Statement, a lot could be analyzed and told to the business owner about the business.

Having a tidy list of depreciable assets, aged accounts receivable, aged accounts payable, and a formal way of counting your inventory, whether it be goods in inventory or work in process inventory. Inventory methods and inventory play a very important part in the outcome of the profit and loss statement.

Modern technology has become a very important factor in running your business. It is likely your industry has software specifically designed to make the business owner's life easy when the owner uses industry specific software. From simple software, word processing, spreadsheets, and databases to complex software that helps tell you when a customer has not been in to see you for a while. Software, hardware, and cloud computing discussions are a big part of running a successful business.

## The Single Owner Business

Here is a situation for a Harvard study and research project. It does not matter the business: carpet store, computer manufacturer, golf course, restaurant, camera store, grocery store. These stores often have an owner, and the owner spends day after day in the store. They are doing the same thing over and over again. Open at 7 am, have coffee at 10 am, lunch with their buddies at noon, then golf at 4 pm.

Or some similar pattern. They come to work and go home from work, and business growth and expansion is not on their mind. It may be one of their hopes. Common to these businesses is that there is no marketing department. The owner is in charge, and what the owner says goes, and the employees follow.

I attended a seminar, and the discussion leader explained that owning a small business was like climbing a mountain. If you start at the bottom and work your way up the mountain at three-quarters of the way up the mountain, then you meet its rock walls then begin scaling them. Then, after a high-altitude walk up a narrow, flimsy staircase, you will reach the top of the mountain. Yeah, you reached the top of the mountain and attained the goal.

Then, it was explained that some of the people start a business and go up the mountain, and at the first rest stop, they spend the next 30 years never reaching or approaching the top of the mountain.

This is how uninformed business people do when they start their business. They design systems and procedures due to bad experiences in their own business. Some would call this seat-of-the-pants management; only doing something if a rock falls on your head! They never learn or study the industry standards for systems and procedures for their type of business.

They get everything going so that the money is coming in and the money is going out, and there is a little bit to take home. Then, they stop learning and stop growing the business. They have no system for getting new customers; they just wait and wait, hoping that someone will find them. If you suggest advertising, they say no because advertising is expensive.

So "mom and pop" shops, there are many in the United States. I often wondered, for each business there is in the whole country, what if I injected $4 million into the business? What could we grow this mom-and-pop shop into?

Mom and Pop can do the research themselves. They need to take online or community college classes to constantly improve their many needed business skills. Then, they find a business in a distant city that is ten times larger than their business and study well what they do, how they advertise, and how they attract customers to the business.

What lines of products do they stock on the shelves? Where is the receiving dock? What are their receiving procedures? How do they handle a request for an item they don't carry in the store?

Thoroughly examine this distant business and then go back and try to make your business look more like their business. Every business that does not advertise or have a marketing function will never reach the top of the mountain. Your business needs to fire on all ten cylinders. You can use this same study pattern for a law office, dental office, doctor's office, restaurant, beauty salon, or e-commerce store.

You, too, can wonder what would happen if SBA gave your business a $4 million loan to expand; what exactly would you, the owner, do? Likely nothing. The owner is trapped. They will not get out from behind the counter. They do not have the mindset of an entrepreneur.

They will not let or trust the employees to run the business, because their belief is: only they can do this. It is well beyond their skill level to start a second store, as this would call for managerial talents and skills. In other words, they are stuck in their path on the side of the road. They make ends meet to keep the doors open but have not got a plan, idea, training, or the inclination to open a second location.

They are frozen in their tracks because they have never grown a business before. They have never started a business and risen to the executive level before. It's the unknown that they are afraid of. For some people, it is what you don't know that is holding you back. The old saying, "You don't know what you don't know!"

This fear of the unknown has them frozen in their tracks because they are comfortable; they can buy food and drive a nice car. Over time you will learn that what you don't know is the roadblock to your future success.

It's easy to learn the next steps because we are a management consulting firm specializing in small and medium-sized businesses. We help businesses grow; therefore, the steps and procedures are known to us, and we can teach you how to grow your own business. We have done this over and over again. It is our job!

You don't have to take a four-year course. Because schools and universities do not teach classes on how to grow your business. We have done this over and over and over again and know the steps and know the process and layout for our clients the next steps. We cannot do the steps for them, but we can offer a clear explanation as to what to do. It's up to the business owner to heed the advice and take the steps in the right direction for future business growth.

You did the right thing; you broke away from the 8 to 5 job and took the risk to start a business. You have a business because sales are being made, vendors are being paid, and that is it, end of the line—we don't need to learn anymore.

My study of this situation shows that these owners need to be retrained in how to do what they are doing at an "executive" level. Many of these owners are college graduates and light up at the idea of being an executive but refuse to install systems or marketing that will bring more customers in the door or offer an incentive to the existing customers to come back.

The thought of sitting at a desk and managing ten stores is a warm thought, but nope, they are going to hold tightly onto the reins and keep doing what they are doing with no desire to begin the steps of transition from shop keeper of one store to executive level owner manager operating ten stores.

The Federal Government has the SBA to loan you money; if you are credit worthy, then you have to qualify. But there is no Czar of business growth and expansion showing existing businesses how to grow into other store locations or sprout a new line of business into the existing stores to better utilize the space and cause the retail "pulse recorder"—revenue per square foot—to go up.

If you start a business unprepared, you will fail. There are a lot of entrepreneurial business failures, mostly because they set sail to start a business unprepared and without the proper briefing, information or education. They did not seek out consultants that could be of valuable help. The distance between start-ups and sustainable sales left a gap they could not fill with out-of-pocket savings; they were underfinanced. When you transition to self-employment, you need to be properly prepared, or you need to be like a track star and make the initial sales happen and build a base of customers very quickly.

Many people decide to start a business, and they dive in. Then, they begin to see the obstacles. Because they are resilient, they respond and keep responding. They know the way to a comfortable place is to build the sales. They started the business because they applied for ten credit cards. They are using the credit card money to launch the business. They are dynamic people who appear to be as fit as navy seals as they continue to respond to the daily challenges of business. In the end, they succeed.

Starting a business on a shoestring budget can pose numerous hazards. Limited funds can lead to inadequate marketing efforts, making it difficult to; reach potential customers, making sales then put money in the bank.

Insufficient capital may also hinder hiring skilled staff or investing in necessary equipment. Furthermore, cash flow challenges can arise, jeopardizing day-to-day operations.

In the end, determined entrepreneurs can overcome these obstacles. The business owner can gradually attract customers by adopting a lean approach, carefully managing expenses, and leveraging cost effective marketing strategies like social media and word of mouth.

The business gains traction through the owner's determination, perseverance, creativity, and delivering exceptional value. As revenue increases, the owner reinvests in the company, expands their offerings, and ultimately achieves success.

Starting a business on a shoestring budget is possible, but you have to be able to rise to the occasion and become determined to make it happen. Obviously, if the average person jumps into business this way, this business will likely fail due to insufficient starting capital.

## CHAPTER 7

# Awareness of the Economy and Economic Climate

To run a business, you need to know about the influencing external factors and the environment that you are operating within.

When you mention economics to many, they run the other way! Either they have never taken an economics class, or there are those who took an economics class and survived but never understood what the professor was actually talking about. Then there are the 10% who took the class and understand the principles and are looking for a way to use them when analyzing their business and making decisions about their business.

Taking into your hands a business, selling goods or services to customers, having an understanding of the national and world economy is important.

You will need to know about a wide range of economic indicators that are published daily or weekly.

For example, you need to know what the prime interest rate is. If you have a need to purchase equipment, know in advance where you are going to go to get an equipment loan and how far above the prime interest rate that loan is going to cost.

The prime rate is the interest rate that banks use as a basis (reference point) to set rates for different types of loans, credit cards, or lines of credit. You can never expect a bank to loan you money at the prime rate. You will have to work with your bank to get a favorable percentage above the prime rate. The interest rates the bank charges are based upon the bank's interpretation of your creditworthiness.

The Federal Reserve sets interest rates for Federal Funds, and then banks follow this pattern with a response when setting interest rates. They pay depositors interest income, and then loan the money to businesses. You will need to know what they charge; fees and interest costs for various types of loans the bank makes. There is a direct correlation from the Federal Funds rate and immediate reaction that will trickle down to affect your business's economic situation.

Of course, if you have a 10-year equipment loan at 4%, you need to read your contract to see if the rate is fixed for the term of the contract or if the rate adjusts periodically when the federal funds rate adjusts.

Be alert and aware of economic forecasts and expected trends. Know when 45% of small businesses report increased revenue for the past quarter, 42% of small businesses report increased profitability, 35% of small and medium-sized businesses expect to add additional employees, and when 10% of small and medium sized businesses are planning on decreasing staff. These factors may influence your decisions, such as making some decisions about increasing or decreasing your employee count. Then deciding who can work from home, who has to report to the office building, and who has to be out in the field selling or providing customer service.

Learn the general direction of the economy, whether there is inflation or a recession coming, and what the next six months, 12 months, and 18 months going to bring to your business. Know these things ahead of time. There are several business magazines and economic magazines that keep up with the trends and will provide you with informed forecasts of what the next 18 months might bring. Get your financial news from a reliable source.

A business owner needs also to understand the world market. What is happening with favored trade nations? How does your product fit into this equation? Is the raw material for your finished product coming from a foreign country where shipping times, rates, and arrivals are part of what you need to know to run your business effectively?

If you have no foreign exposure, then your product may fit the niche of "Made in America," which is something you might want to refer to when marketing your product. According to the Federal Trade Commission, "Made in USA" means that "all or virtually all" the product has been made in America. That is, all significant parts, processing, and labor that go into the product must be of U.S. origin.

Courses in economics, when evaluating the various high-level theories, guide a student through the analysis of whether it is better for America to make the products within the borders of the US or what happens if the product is made in other countries and then imported into the US for sale in domestic markets. For most students, you can get lost pretty fast if you try to understand all of the surrounding economic theories and principles. Thus, in this book, I lay out economics in easy to understand language, knowing that there are more complex theories behind these basic principles.

The US dollar exchange rate is important because you might want to go on a vacation or business trip to New Zealand, then you will want to know how much in US dollars a dinner costing $110 New Zealand dollars costs you. What is your out of pocket cost? When the dollar fluctuates, it might make purchasing your product harder for foreign persons.

One needs to understand economics to interpret your business impact when the Dow Jones Industrial Average (DJIA) goes up and what the impact will be if the DJIA goes down. The DJIA is a math calculation when considering the stock price of 30 select companies that have agreed to be part of the DJIA. These same stock prices are measured every day, and it is the same companies being measured every day, giving the world, economic information to make business interpretations. The 30 companies stay the same until there is consensus that a few companies need to be released and new companies need to be entered into the DJIA and provide business owners with a true pulse of the US stock market.

The DJIA is a reference number that tells business owners in a flash of the overall trend in large company's earnings. You have to know are large company earnings going up, or are they going down?

It is important to know that a stock's price is influenced by many factors. Most investors give heavy weight to the earnings of a company when coming to a conclusion as to what the stock price should be on a given day. Some investors understand that a stock may be priced today based upon its future earnings.

If interest rates are high, the DJIA is trending down, and the US dollar value in foreign markets is declining, you must know this is a strong signal that your business sales and your business customer demand may also be going down. To run a business, one has to be aware of common business economic indicators.

When you see in the news: Ships are piling up, and shipping prices are spiking amid a labor fight between port operators and workers, threatening a new round of supply chain disruptions. You will know how to plan your next 12 months in business. Future planning prevents driving the ship (your company) into the rocks.

If one were to press deeper into the stock market and ask what valuable information can be extracted to help you run your business better, you would also consider the other major stock indexes. The S&P 500, Nasdaq Composite, and the Russell 2000.

There are more economic indicators that business owners can watch to know whether it's a good time to expand or to stay static for now, or good judgment might come to a conclusion to contract business operations, weather the storm, and then plan to ramp up under more favorable conditions.

We are learning about supply and demand and how it influences price. Then, the other side of the equation is consumer disposable income. Are the customers poised with extra money to be able to purchase your product? You also need to know well how sensitive your product or service is to fluctuations in the economy.

GDP, Gross Domestic Product, is the market value of all goods and services produced within the US during a certain measured period of time.

Unemployment rate: this might tip you off if it is going to be easy to find employees or if it is going to be difficult to find employees.

CPI, consumer price index. This is the measurement of consumer goods and services. The Consumer Price Index (CPI) measures change over time in the prices paid by consumers for a measured basket of goods and services.

Watch the savings rate in the US, as this indicator will tell one about the discretionary spending capabilities of consumers. A low savings rate points to less money that consumers have to spend on purchases from your company.

Be aware of the price of crude oil for obvious reasons. You want to know if your and your customer's discretionary dollars are going to be eaten up when you take your car to the gas station. Also, you will know what your vendors are contending with when they transport goods to you or their costs of getting the raw materials into their door. Fuel prices have become a political football. If you plug your car in at night, the power company may be purchasing fuel to be able to make the electricity.

Consumer Debt, which includes home mortgages, credit card debt, student loans, car loans, and other personal borrowing. Using money to repay this debt lowers the amount of disposable income used to purchase your company's goods. There may be a correlation between the savings rate and the consumer debt amount that you would want to be aware of. Awareness is important so that you can make good decisions about the direction your company will go during the next six months.

The Department of Labor, the IRS, and other governmental agencies are sensitive to your particular industry and are good to keep in touch with. You can sign up for their free newsletters and watch their websites for important information affecting your business. Some people like to watch the SEC to see who they are chasing, then wait for that company's stock to drop, then make investing decisions.

More important is how to drive the ship through the beginning stages of your company and through turbulent times. Knowing how to improve sales creates teamwork in the production area to produce the product.

Then, troubleshoot the product, assuring that your brand releases quality workmanship into the hands of the customers (quality control). The quality of your product must be protected by you to ensure what is on your mind and what works out in small batches is exactly the product that is going onto store shelves and then into the consumers hands.

This step is further complicated by food safety programs and the regulatory and governmental agencies affecting your business, being sure that your product does not contain or come in contact with contaminates that could tarnish your brand or cause the product to do something unexpected once sitting in the sealed can or packaged and on a shelf for 60 days.

One has to understand US economics to be able to know when to expand, when to keep things the same, or when to expect a downturn in your business sales.

Construction companies' furniture stores are often affected by changes or downturns in the economy. You do not want to launch a growth campaign while the overall economy is going downhill. The computer parts supply business is a bit more stable in that big changes to the economy, up or down, do not affect this industry very much. Month by month it is important to know how your company stacks up when compared to the present economic conditions.

Plastic surgeons suffer during steep downturns of the economy, while some law firms thrive during economic downturns. To know the economic environment is important.

There are some basic principles coming from the study of economics. Supply and Demand drive the price of your product or service. Are you in a business, and do you produce a product that is in short supply? If so, you may be able to ask for a higher price for your product. This is the value of the free market. The principles of supply and demand are part of everyday business. Supply and demand work. This is not a theory in a laboratory, it is time tested in the marketplace. There is no room for government intervention because it has proven to only goof up the principles of supply and demand.

If you are in a business and produce a product that has a surplus in the marketplace and your product is the same as other competitors, then there will be little demand for your product. Thus, the sales price for your product or service will likely have to be reduced in order to influence consumers to purchase your product.

The economic theories of supply and demand influence the price at which you can sell your goods and services.

You have to see the value in making the consumer happy so that they will tell their friends and family about your product. Word of mouth marketing is one of the most important secrets in marketing products or services.

Marketing, advertising, public relations, innovation, quality control, engineering, production, purchasing, payroll, bookkeeping, record retention, accounting management, team building, leadership… These are the many hats of the entrepreneur. If you are new to any of these subject areas, then there are consultants in the marketplace, familiar with your product line, who are ready, willing, and able to help you.

Many schools have developed courses in entrepreneurship that study what Henry Ford did in 1909. This is what I hated most about my college level entrepreneurship class. None of the class was dedicated to forward thinking of what to do to start a business. What are the risks, and what are the obstacles? Tell me in advance what I have to do, what do I need to know?

What skills do I need, and what talent and knowledge do I need to possess? The class was a list of case studies where people started a business that succeeded from 1900 to 1942. None of this class suggested the type of dedication and determination that one needs to be an entrepreneur. No people skills, social skills, or self-improvement suggestions were made. The class just studied people who assumed the risk, and it succeeded by the way Henry Ford made a production line that made common sense.

In this book, I hope to break the mold and show people how to escape their 8 to 5 jobs and sweat every two weeks that they did not get fired. In corporate America, you have to give up 30% or more of your check to taxes, whereas, in self-employment, you don't get fired unless you go broke; you don't go broke if you have good management skills.

In self-employment you can enjoy a life of freedom and flexibility. There is not one college graduate who cannot succeed in self-employment as an entrepreneur. Many lack the belief, courage, and support network to overcome their fears of failure to accept the challenge of survival as a business owner.

Entrepreneurs are self-employed people. Becoming self-employed is a desired destination. A self-employed person refers to any person who earns their living from any independent pursuit of economic activity as opposed to earning a living working for a company or another individual (an employer). Sally, a self-employed e-commerce platform person, won her freedom and said, "No one can tell me what to do because I am the BOSS! I am in charge of my own future."

People choose to become self-employed for many reasons, including greater independence and flexibility. If you stick with it and learn what you need to know to survive, your income will likely be three times or more than if you stayed at the 8 to 5 job.

For many self-employed people, autonomy is a big reward: the freedom and flexibility to do what you want, when you want. While being self-employed, you are able to make your own decisions, hopefully informed decisions. Some people find joy in starting a new business and watching it grow. There has been a surge in self-employment since 2008.

Entrepreneurship classes study the early American "pioneer." Still today, the organized, methodical, speed oriented production line exists today. However, Henry did not consider the automation of the production line or the skillful use of robots.

Schools are missing the boat by not training qualified soldiers to enter the business of start-up and survival, self-employment. Many business schools discuss venture capital, and students leave thinking that their company can be started and survive by taking on new loans and taking on more investors to continually fund the checkbook while the entrepreneur tries to build a company that can earn a profit.

Profit is the focus because tomorrow and keeping the doors open happens only if profit is present. Profit is "new money" earnings for the business to save and spend wisely to ensure there is a tomorrow for the company.

A business is not built because of a business plan. A business is built with a business plan, a good plan that contains enough flexibility to respond quickly to the needs of the customers and to improve the product so more profit becomes available.

The financing business plan is different from the operating business plan. Once the business is started, you should draft a quarterly plan of operations that keeps you focused on improving the company. The financing business plan has to tell a compelling story. It has to be weighted down with facts and figures.

The compelling story and the facts and figures are what are going to perk interest in the investors looking at your business plan. You can't just sit down and say you hope or dream this will happen; you have to tell a compelling story backed up by facts and figures that will cause the investor to reach for their checkbook first, and then they can ask questions later. You have to build into the presentation credibility and enthusiasm, then sell your ability to execute the plan.

**The main components of a financing business plan are seven elements:**

1. Summary, in a nutshell, overall summary
2. Company description, key employees, management team
3. Description and function of products and services
4. Market analysis, identifying your target market
5. Marketing strategy
6. Financials and budget
7. Appendix

You will also want to include an appendix that contains data and sources supporting the main sections. This has to be supported by facts and not just pages of hot air.

The traditional business plan contains formal documents that lay out the goals for the business, how owners plan to achieve those goals, and how much time they anticipate they will need to achieve them. How much money is needed, and how much money will be left over after a designated period of time?

In this plan, you will want to make the case that there is an experienced, educated management team. You will want to lay out how the investor dollars are going to be utilized. You have to explain the road to profitability and how quickly you will get onto that road.

A business plan presented to venture capital (VC) investors is a strategic document designed to outline the key elements of a startup or early-stage company's business model, growth strategy, and potential for financial success. It serves as a comprehensive roadmap that communicates the company's value proposition, market opportunity, execution plans, and financial projections. Typically spanning around 20-30 pages, the business plan is crucial in capturing the attention and interest of VC investors who seek high potential opportunities for investment.

The business plan begins with an executive summary, providing a concise briefing and overview of the company's mission, product or service offering, target market, and competitive advantage. It should spark the investor's curiosity and provide a glimpse into the venture's potential.

The plan then delves into market analysis, demonstrating a deep understanding of the industry landscape, market trends, and customer needs. Competitive analysis highlights key players and their strengths, showcasing how the company differentiates itself.

The document outlines the company's product or service in detail, including its unique selling points and how it addresses market gaps. The go to market strategy reveals how the company plans to reach customers, acquire users, and scale its operations efficiently.

Financial projections are a critical component, offering a multi-year outlook on revenue, expenses, and profitability. This section provides investors with a glimpse into the company's growth trajectory and potential return on investment. These projections need to be reasonable.

Operational and organizational details describe the company's internal structure, management team, and roles. Investors want assurance that the team has the experience and skills necessary to execute the business plan successfully.

A comprehensive marketing and sales strategy showcases how the company plans to attract and retain customers. This includes customer acquisition channels, pricing strategies, and plans for customer engagement.

Risks and mitigation strategies demonstrate the company's awareness of potential challenges and its preparedness to address them. This transparency builds investor confidence in the venture's resilience. It is here that you would identify nearby competition.

The business plan also highlights milestones and key performance indicators that serve as checkpoints for tracking progress. This helps investors assess the company's execution against its stated goals.

A business plan tailored for VC investors encapsulates a startup's vision, strategy, market analysis, financial projections, team expertise, and risk mitigation strategies. Its purpose is to captivate investor interest, provide a clear roadmap for growth, and instill confidence in the startup's potential for success in a competitive market.

People who run their company for eight years, never producing a profit (Amazon), are defying the odds of survival. Most non-profitable companies will fail, fold, and go out of business.

Many people from large universities leave thinking that, my bright idea will get quickly funded with venture capital. Then, with that capital, I will set in motion the idea and work out the kinks as they come.

In analyzing this thesis on the surface, it is correct. But nowhere has profit been mentioned, and at no time was profit the focus of the work week. Profit is your key to freedom.

With profit, you do not need more investors while giving up 40% of the ownership of your idea, product, or service. Get some funding to get into business, then be in a race to get to profitability, and then remain the

100% owner of your company. Build sales, expand operations, then go public and cash in for a big payday when you sell your stock as an IPO.

If you go with the negative cash flow style for five years, then look around, you no longer own 100% of the company anymore. The venture capital people own the company. When your ownership percentage goes below 51%, then you are in bad shape because you, too, could be tossed out of your own company, the company you founded. Having less than 51% of the company, you have lost the total CONTROL of the company, so never let yourself get into this position. Even the TV Shark Tank cast understands this situation.

The best way to get off to a solid start is to pay back the loans and advances to retain/regain 100% ownership of the company you founded. This is easily done when you are year after year earning more profits. Adopt profits as a focus and mindset, then make plans that protect your abilities to make a profit.

Often, in talking with people starting out as new entrepreneurs, we point out that technology and software development have produced many new entrepreneurs from 2000 to 2020.

The college student who is six months away from graduation feels tension about what will be the job in the workforce they will have to undertake. They start asking if they will be happy. Can they get married and raise a family, buy a house and tons of jewelry for the wife? Or do you remain single, find the right business to be the founder of, scale it to profitability, then get married and buy the house? There are a lot of decisions to make. Where you set your priorities is important.

All this thought process and pressure forces a student or group of students to band together and create a website or app that fills a gap in society. They design the product, launch it, make sure it works, and then market it, all of this done before June graduation.

Then, over the summer, the product gains traffic and momentum, so they still don't have to go get jobs. Then, by December, they sell the software, website, or app to a larger company for $6 million. Whew, now they can take a break from having to go look for a job!!

Knowing about foreign markets is also important for the seasoned medium sized entrepreneurs. What is selling well in America may also sell well in Canada, England, South America, Western Europe, and possibly the Asian markets.

Entrepreneurs want to avoid tunnel vision and want to keep their periscope up for the possibility of selling the same product to foreign markets. Sometimes, products need to be adjusted slightly to fit into a foreign market due to cultural differences, but many times, these shifts are minor as you try to fit the product into a different market or different culture.

Many times, the "made in America" or "enjoyed in California" pitch to a foreign market gives one a great competitive advantage.

Overcoming cultural differences with an American made product offers several benefits. It allows for effective communication and understanding between the American company and foreign customers, leading to stronger relationships and increased customer satisfaction.

It promotes cultural exchange and appreciation, fostering goodwill and mutual respect. Moreover, an American made product can symbolize quality, reliability, and adherence to stringent standards, instilling confidence in foreign market consumers.

Selling these products in foreign markets brings immense joy as it opens doors to new opportunities, expands the customer base, and boosts revenue. It also enhances the company's reputation internationally, leading to potential partnerships and collaborations.

However, conducting business in a foreign country that may not respect your Louisiana contract comes with hazards. The lack of contract enforcement may result in breaches of the agreement, non-payment, or legal disputes. Different legal systems and cultural norms can also pose challenges, making it essential to navigate unfamiliar territory carefully.

Language barriers, logistical issues, and trade barriers could further complicate operations. Cultural differences and business practices may require additional efforts to build trust and negotiate successfully. It is crucial to conduct thorough research, establish local partnerships, and seek legal advice to mitigate these hazards and protect your company's interests in foreign markets.

**CHAPTER 8**

# Networking, Branching Out, and Leadership

There are groups and organizations that help entrepreneurs succeed. Investigate your industry and find the annual convention of decorated cupcake makers. Look to your local Chamber of Commerce, the NFIB organization, and the representative for your area.

Look to the American Management Association and University programs that would be helpful to your product or service. The university library will contain a wealth of information for you to research and learn more about your products or services.

Networking is a term in the marketplace that is valuable but under practiced by many. Not often can the lone wolf make it to the top solo. You have to begin forming a circle of friends. Those friends have friends that can be helpful to the success of your business.

Business networking is the process of establishing and nurturing relationships with other professionals, vendors, competitors, friends, politicians, bankers, and companies to exchange information, resources, and opportunities. For a company owner, networking is valuable as it opens doors to potential partnerships, clients, and industry insights, facilitating growth and success.

Networking is about interacting and engaging with people for mutual benefit. Being a participant in a "mastermind" group is networking on steroids. Mastermind groups are small groups of ten or fewer members, all meeting similar challenges in business. You meet in person, share your challenges, and listen—yes, listen to the group feedback on how to solve or find the solution for your present day challenges.

If you are facing challenges in your business, your networking group may be able to provide you with information and feedback or put you in touch with someone who is an expert who can help. When you network, you make yourself available to help others in your network solve their problems or challenges.

You need to have a contact list or CRM database of people in your network who can provide information, advice, or influence in making your company run more smoothly. Your network may not have formal meetings, but one on one, having lunch with members of your network or spending time calling them on the phone will help keep these people alive and lively in your network, available to help you conquer the next challenge that business presents.

When you mention networking to some people, they cringe and shy away. To others, it sounds like a party that they don't want to miss. There is a vastly different reaction in the business marketplace to the concept of networking.

Let me be the first to tell you that your success in business depends upon your networking abilities. If you have built a strong network, there are a lot of people in your inner circle to converse with to gain ideas and direction. Networking can be done to build your business or to build your social network, gaining friends with common interests to have fun with and to laugh with all year long.

Social media offers a not so intimate form of networking, and many times, you don't know the real credentials of the person on the other end.

Your network has to be more intimate, and you need to have the ability to sit with people in private and have a conversation. Video conferencing has greatly improved opportunities to network with busy people. If your network is known to each other, a Slack channel could be an avenue to toss out a question or challenge and get a lot of powerful feedback within a short period of time.

Networking is a process that fosters the exchange of information and ideas among individuals or groups that share a common interest. Networking tests your ability to meet new people. It is a showing of the development of your social skills. Some people want to know and go through life with the same ten people. Other people are interested in building empires. These people have a strong social and business network, assembled by work steps, that involves reaching out to meet new people.

Some people set a business goal of meeting ten new people a week. These people find social and business motives for networking. Your sales force should have a specific target of meeting so many new people per week.

Successful networking involves regularly engaging and following up with contacts in the network to provide and receive valuable information that is not readily available outside the network.

Most humans like to interact with other humans. Networking and finding common ground helps satisfy this human need. People like to be recognized, so the head of the network may be looked upon as a leader. Gender difference studies show that women are better at networking than men.

Many people are reserved and afraid to meet new people. Your business survival may be based upon your ability to meet new people. These reserved people seem to be the underperformers. These more reserved people can hire nice looking, over-the-top, energetic people who can make the required marketing calls for them.

Building your connections will provide you with an invaluable opportunity to best prepare for your career goals. It is important to remember that networking is a mutually beneficial process. You never know when your skills and resources can prove to be beneficial and, thus, helpful to others in your network.

In today's world, networking is a necessity. A mountain of research shows that professional networks lead to more jobs and business opportunities, broader and deeper knowledge, improved capacity to innovate, faster advancement, and greater status and authority. Building and nurturing professional relationships also improves the quality of work and increases job satisfaction.

Most people have a dominant motivational focus—what psychologists refer to as either a "promotion" or a "prevention" mindset. Those in the promotion mindset think primarily about the growth, advancement, and accomplishments that networking can bring them, while those in the prevention mindset see it as something they are obligated to take part in for professional reasons.

Promotion focused people network because they want to approach the activity with excitement, curiosity, and an open mind about all the possibilities that might unfold.

Prevention focused people see networking as a necessary evil and feel unauthentic while engaged in it, so they do it less often and as a result, underperform in all aspects of their jobs.

Networking is a socioeconomic business activity by which business people and entrepreneurs meet to form business relationships and to recognize, create, or act upon business opportunities, share information, and seek potential partners for ventures or opportunities.

Networking is worth doing the right way. Try to meet as many people as possible, and come equipped to talk and exchange ideas. It's a good idea to read some jokes online before you go. Then, take a look at major news and financial news and take some interesting facts to share with others. The best way to meet someone is to ask questions. Some people respond well when you ask questions about them or their accomplishments. People always like to share information about themselves.

Networking allows for sharing ideas, thoughts, and feelings, a way of sharing your experiences or challenges and having the advantage of others offering ideas that might help solve problems. Give your insight, which could lead to meeting a new contact that can become a customer of your business. Cultivating personal relationships and creating a helpful resource and network of people to share ideas with or gain business ideas or referrals from can be helpful.

Networking boils down to being an exercise in relationship building. This is done by strategically reaching out to make contact with other people. This can easily be done by hiking, tennis, golf, and other activities. Your network grows if you have someone in your network introduce you to another person or if you take the initiative by inviting someone new to lunch to compare notes and accomplishments with. Remember that going to lunch, hiking, tennis, golf, and all other activities, if done with the proper business purpose, may be tax deductible.

At Canberra Company, we make a point to help and train our clients in how to network. We analyze what method of networking will work comfortably for you, and we follow up to see that you are meeting your goals that have been mutually established. We have a proven track record of enhancing the performance of manufacturers, hospitality, realtors, marketing personnel, farmers, ranchers, winery operators, contractors, and several other industries.

We are happy to introduce our clients to our network of business, medical, legal, restaurant, and political giants across the country who have been quite helpful in the past years. Getting plugged in may be helpful to your business.

Remember, networking is about sharing information. Networking can help form and keep valuable relationships with people to obtain free advice on how to overcome business challenges.

Business networking is a way of leveraging your business and personal connections to help you bring in new customers and vendors or to get great advice for running your business.

Don't be bashful about this. I have helped small groups of CEOs who meet similar challenges in running public companies. They meet with each other by video conference, then annually meet in a designated spot to have lunch and share experiences gained during the year and to personally thank the members of the network who are also CEOs, where all understand that their time is valuable.

Your goal is to achieve business success through the use of collaborative relationships.

Networking is a crucial element in running an entrepreneurial business, playing a pivotal role in achieving success through collaborative relationships. Effective networking allows entrepreneurs to expand their reach, tap into new markets, and gain valuable insights and knowledge. By establishing connections with like-minded individuals, entrepreneurs can access a wealth of resources, including potential clients, suppliers, and mentors.

Collaborative relationships formed through networking create opportunities for partnership, joint ventures, and shared learning. These relationships enable entrepreneurs to pool their strengths, skills, and expertise, fostering innovation and problem solving. Moreover, networking provides a platform for sharing experiences, challenges, and best practices, allowing entrepreneurs to learn from one another and avoid common pitfalls.

Networking also enhances visibility and credibility within the industry. By building a strong professional network, entrepreneurs can gain referrals, recommendations, and endorsements, leading to increased brand recognition and customer trust.

Networking is invaluable to entrepreneurs as it facilitates collaboration, access to resources, knowledge sharing, and increased visibility, ultimately driving business success in an increasingly interconnected world.

## The Advanced Entrepreneur

Someone who has been the owner of a business, grew the business, and then attended more school to become an MBA may take a different approach to entrepreneurship. They have the confidence, ambition, drive, determination, and belief in themselves, they know business methods, and they like building businesses. These people would seek out businesses to purchase.

Their hunt for an available business may stretch far and wide. They may be working with four regional business brokers, and then, much like a rabid real estate professional looking for listings, they would search for a business that is in need of a purchaser. These businesses may offer a good product or service, but the owners are not running the business very well, and they refuse to hire professional help. They would be a likely target for purchase. The advanced entrepreneur would size up the business and make the owners a purchase offer.

The advanced entrepreneur's objective is to purchase the business based on today's annual sales and other business valuation factors. Once purchased, the advanced entrepreneur would get qualified employees into the business to fill certain roles. Then, the idea is to grow the business bigger by analyzing the current position, and then, through marketing efforts and improved production efforts, the entrepreneur would grow the business to have 10 to 20 times the annual sales. This process may take five years to accomplish.

All along, the advanced entrepreneur had in mind when purchasing this business to eventually sell the business. This advanced entrepreneur researched three likely candidates who would be interested in purchasing this business later down the road.

The advanced entrepreneur developed and grew the business in such a way as to be more appealing to his recently researched companies five years down the line when the advanced entrepreneur forecasted the sale of the business.

The business was grown to be a perfect fit into one of the target acquiring businesses. This was the advanced entrepreneur's plan. Buy the business. Develop the business, then sell the business. By following this path, the entrepreneur could have purchased the business for $300,000 and, in turn, sold the business after it was carefully built for $10 million. As you can see, there is a handsome profit.

The entrepreneur is now in a position to start the process all over again. Many people across the country make their living by purchasing existing businesses, using their own knowledge, skills, and tools to build the business, and then selling the business to a perfectly fit suitor.

They have identified the suitor either before or within 60 days of completing the purchase.

You can see what happened. The first owner was able to get the business up and running but lacked the skills to grow the business. Someone with more skills purchased the business, then, using good business tactics, built the business up, built a team of qualified employees, and then had the knowledge and communication skills to sell the business to a fairly large corporation.

Grocery store shelves are lined with products that could have evolved this way. This recipe does not just apply to consumer goods; the same formula applies to every industry in existence today.

Advanced entrepreneurs come in many shapes and sizes. Take, for example, the Driscoll Strawberry Company. They started out as a farming company growing strawberries, then over time, became a strawberry marketing giant.

They had many farmers growing the fruit that Driscoll supplied the seeds or small plants, and then the farmer grew the fruit. The farmer was obligated by contract to deliver the fruit when harvested to a Driscoll strawberry cooling facility. Driscol put their brand on the product and then sold the product to high-end Hotels and Restaurants. Big, red, beautiful berries with the correct texture, taste, and smell to please the most decerning pallet.

How did they do this?? This is a family owned business. Great grandpa started, and then Grandpa took over. Grandpa was wise and found scientists who knew how to develop the seedlings of the strawberry plant. Grandpa hired the scientists to work for the Driscoll Company. Through field trial and error, these scientists developed the most perfect strawberry seed. One with proper taste and texture, the size was perfect, and the shelf life was long. Having a long shelf life for perishable inventory is a major win.

This unique family story goes on and on about how a family from one generation to the next can prosper. The next generation is groomed to do something, such as studying, learning, and how to add value to the company that will make better the Driscoll brand.

Going to work for your parents after becoming well educated is a challenge for the child and the parent. This difficulty launched the "succession planning" industry. Lawyers, accountants, insurance agents, bankers, and psychologists are now taught and take continuing education classes in "succession planning" and the art and mechanics of how a company is passed from one generation to the next generation.

The children have to get in touch with their core values and beliefs and become willing to learn how to achieve. At Canberra Company, we are the trainers of families on how to pass the business down from one generation to the next.

Then, once employing the children at the executive level, both the parents and the children have to take classes and training on how to cope with this transition from child to executive, the future leader of the company.

I will tell everyone in advance this is no easy task, and families struggle with this. From the moment the child is born, working in the family business is the dream for the parent. On the other hand, the child begins normally and naturally striving for independence at around age 12 or 13. Independence and working for your parents do not belong in the same sentence.

From a psychological point of view, this is where the tug of war begins.

I will have another book dedicated to "family business succession planning" to lay out on the canvas the entire problem, the pitfalls, common errors, and the formula to accomplish the result that everyone wants.

There is a national statistic saying that not many family owned businesses pass down to the third generation. It's the third generation that has gone to the city or another country to get a job to show off their uniqueness.

Some families bluntly tell the children they are too lazy to learn all the ropes of running a sizable business. It's the third generation that inherits the stock of the company and then soon after holds a meeting announcing the sale of the business to another company, likely a competitor, for millions or billions of dollars.

Succession planning is the deliberate and strategic process of identifying and developing individuals within an organization to assume key leadership roles in the future.

The polished art of succession planning involves meticulous attention to detail, thoughtful analysis, and effective implementation. It requires a comprehensive understanding of the organization's current and future needs, as well as the capabilities and potential of potential successors.

The process involves identifying high potential individuals, providing them with the necessary training and development opportunities, and gradually transitioning them into leadership positions. Effective succession planning also includes regular evaluation and adjustment of the plan to align with changing circumstances and organizational goals. By mastering the art of succession planning, organizations can ensure a seamless leadership transition, maintain continuity and foster long term success.

Bear in mind that effective estate planning can prevent the disaster, the selling of the company. Many families don't take the time or have the courage to learn from knowledgeable estate planners how to keep the company going. They can put restrictions on the stock given to beneficiaries, but they don't because this act would deny the children once the parent has gone to the grave!! Estate planning is important and succession planning is important. The two go hand in hand in preserving the longevity of the company.

Succession planning would, after graduation from college and a few years of working as an employee for another company, then recruit some or all of the children to work for the family business. With some families, we hold an annual draft like the NFL or the NBA and send invitations to the educated family members who might make good team players. This is most effective when you have three brothers who started the company, and each of them had four or five children, all of similar age! Some of the children went to college, and others did not. Some of the cousins get along well, and others do not. One can begin to see where the complications appear!

The children would be taught they have to make a contribution to the company, become part of the team, and do credible things that would give them an easy path to an executive role with the company. Parents and children have to know the past has been a child parent relationship. This is now, going forward, an employer-employee relationship. The objective is to give the children a chance to prove themselves capable of taking the reins and later, when called upon, run the company.

The parents have to give up a tight grip on the reins of the company and let the child executive have a supervised turn in the driver's seat so that they get used to the manner and method of running the company.

Open communication, transparency, and clear expectations are crucial when dealing with the succession planning of the child parent relationship transitioning to the executive employee-employer relationship.

It is important for both parties to have honest conversations about roles, responsibilities, and goals. Establishing a formal transition plan outlining the timeline and steps involved can provide clarity and minimize potential conflicts.

Identifying areas for skill development, providing training or mentoring opportunities, and gradually increasing the child's responsibilities can aid in a smooth transition. Regular feedback and evaluation processes can ensure ongoing alignment and growth within the executive-employer relationship. Both sides need to take steps to gain acceptance from the non-family member employees.

An example of this is the William Wrigley Jr. Company, a huge all-American, pioneer, entrepreneurial success story. A company that went from the street corner to a huge worldwide company selling billions of dollars of chewing gum. The third generation sold the company to the competition, the Mars Company.

Let's get back to the Driscoll Company making strawberry industry history. Why did the Driscoll Company have success? They solved a problem; they grew unique fruit with an extended shelf life. They developed the plant at the scientific level, and thus, the competition could not get the same rootstock to be able to compete.

They had customer satisfaction as an obsession. Obsession is well beyond a priority!! The scientific employees gave them a competitive edge. Having a competitive edge has proven to be very profitable for many companies. The Driscoll Company built a brand that stood for quality. The consumer demanded the product, forcing Hotels and Restaurants to buy the product at a decent price.

The Driscoll Company enjoys satisfaction, seeing their fruit in high demand.

Running a medium sized company is not an easy task. It takes time to build, and it takes a leader with skills to find, groom, and train qualified, competent employees. You have to exercise modern skills to manage the company. One has to oversee the proper marketing of the product with a sloped line graphed upward due to increased annual sales.

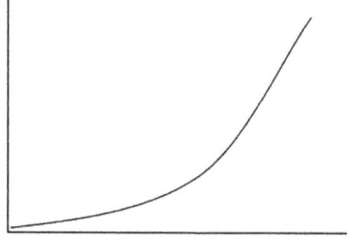

It takes a talented crew of employees to produce the product or service according to modern cutting edge standards. Then, you have to surround yourself with knowledgeable people and consultants who can shape and grow a company. Let them assist you in the further development of the business. The business is not going to grow because Grandpa said so.

The business is going to grow because current day management is going to make decisions on how to guide the company into an evolving, ever changing, and modernizing future. A future of technology, modern methods, and better tools to streamline company operations and position itself for continued growth into the future with evolving social patterns.

## Multi-Unit Operations

Much of the study of entrepreneurship is about the single owner of one location. To open other locations takes a whole new look at your business.

We are premier consultants to the restaurant business and tell everyone starting in the restaurant business that they are not going to make a comfortable living until they have four stores.

With the fourth store, your annual income, the owner's take home pay, becomes $400,000 or more per year, depending on how efficient your store operations are.

Having multiple units means that you have to have a sound management system, a sound accounting system, good internal controls, seasoned marketing steps, and customer satisfaction.

Taking a single owner from one store into four stores is very difficult work because the owner is required to think differently, see the business in a different light with adjusted vision, and have the ability to let go and let the employees do their given jobs.

Then, once they have four stores, this is not only proof of concept; it is proof of a functioning management team now poised to grow from 4 to 40 stores. At the 40 store level, the owner's take home pay should be around $3.8 million per year. You would need to work long and hard at an 8-5 job to rise to the management level to be able to take home $3.8 million per year. I can assure you that growing a business to 40 stores is much easier than coping with climbing the ladder in corporate America.

My next book on entrepreneurship will be about multi-unit operations. Watch our web site as we may release a special report that will provide some vital information about this topic.

The most difficult part of having multiple locations is getting the owner away from daily hands on tasks and into the mindset of an executive. An illustration of this is you have to get the "owner cook" out of the kitchen. Sometimes, you have to pry the owner away from daily operations. This can be a difficult task because they hold on so tightly to the reins. Many of these single store owners feel that only they can do the job correctly. This owner has to be ready to shift to the executive mindset.

In the dynamic world of business, growth, and expansion, having multiple locations is essential for long term success. When contemplating the opening of a second location, one critical aspect to consider is the role of the business owner.

Often, owners find themselves consumed by daily tasks, which hinders their ability to focus on strategic planning and broader business goals. However, by stepping back and delegating responsibilities to employees, owners can unlock the true growth potential of their multi-unit operations.

Delegation is not just about offloading tasks; it is a powerful tool for nurturing talent and fostering a sense of ownership among employees. By entrusting capable individuals with important responsibilities, owners empower their team to step up, take charge, and contribute to the success of the business. This not only lightens the owner's workload but also creates a culture of growth, teamwork, and accountability within the organization.

Stepping back from daily tasks allows business owners to shift their focus toward strategic planning and expansion. With more time on their hands, owners can conduct market research, explore new opportunities, and devise effective strategies for the second location. By devoting attention to long term vision and growth, owners can ensure the sustainability and scalability of their multi-unit business.

When employees are given the opportunity to handle crucial tasks and make decisions, it fosters a sense of empowerment and professional development. They feel valued, trusted, and motivated to contribute their best efforts. This, in turn, with more locations, boosts morale and enhances employee loyalty. By empowering employees, owners create a strong foundation for the successful operation of multiple units, even in their absence.

Stepping back and delegating tasks demonstrates trust in the capabilities of the team. This trust is reciprocated by employees, who, in turn, feel a heightened sense of responsibility and dedication. To the employee, their job has become more meaningful. Building a culture of trust creates an environment where employees take ownership of their work, collaborate effectively, and strive for excellence. It also allows the business owner to foster a supportive leadership style that inspires and motivates the team.

While stepping back, business owners can assume a mentorship role. By providing guidance, sharing expertise, and mentoring key employees, owners ensure a smooth transition of responsibilities. Through mentoring, owners can help groom future leaders who can confidently handle day to day operations and even take charge of additional locations. Mentorship strengthens the organizational structure, promotes professional growth, and facilitates the growth of the business as a whole.

In the realm of multi-unit business operations, expanding to a second location presents exciting opportunities for growth. By stepping back and delegating tasks to employees, business owners can leverage their time and expertise to focus on strategic planning and expansion. This approach fosters a culture of empowerment, trust, and accountability within the organization. By nurturing talent, empowering employees, and assuming a mentorship role, business owners pave the way for a thriving multi-unit business poised for long-term success.

Most any business is suited to have multiple locations. In each industry, the choices are different; manufacturing is different than operating dental offices. Each industry needs to be looked at with the idea of what is the reason for having a next location.

Is this going to help the company grow? Is your marketing team ready to gather new customers in the new location? Likely you will have the same vendors?

For some vendors, when the business crosses state lines, then another vendor might be needed. Manufacturing typically but not always located near where the raw materials are, then they look at the logistics of how they are going to get the product out of the plant into the hands of the distributor or retailer.

Opening more locations requires planning and capital. Because of this, the benefits need to be determined in advance of making the shift to open a new location.

A new location means spending more money on rent, utilities, insurance, marketing, staff, supplies, inventory, equipment, tech, and more. It also means your focus will be split between your new responsibilities and your old ones.

While your new location requires a lot of your attention, it's critical that you pay attention to your current business operations so that nothing slips through the cracks.

On a more positive note, consider the opportunities. Opening multiple locations raises your company profile and introduces you to new customers and additional markets. Hopefully, it also leads to increased sales and profits. This is the key. During the growth stage, the profits will go down. Once the new addition is stabilized, the opportunities for new and bigger profits begin to occur.

This information was gathered from the SBA sources and offers good suggestions about what to consider when opening a new location.

- Consider these questions:

- Does your business have a steady cash flow?

- Have you been profitable for at least three years?

- Do you have enough financial resources to support your current location and fund expansion? It's likely that, at first, your new place won't earn enough money to cover your overhead right away. So, sales from your existing business will have to support that, too.

- Is your current business running smoothly? How hands on are you? Can your business afford for you not to be around? For how long?

Do you have a reliable team in place to keep your current location humming? Is there someone you can rely on to take charge? Your employees must be ready to run the existing company without having you around all the time since you'll be spending much of your time at the new location/s.

Is there a demand for your products or services that your current location can't meet? Are you planning to replicate your business in this new location? If so, are you certain a second location won't cannibalize sales from your current business?

Are the consumers similar in your new area, or will you need to alter your offerings to cater to this demographic? Are you prepared to do that?

Here is where expansions often fall down. As you move across the US, there are slightly different cultures, tastes, and different types of social gatherings. Many Texas restaurant chains have fallen by the wayside because they won't/refuse to adjust the product to fit the needs of the culture they expanded into. Often, adjustments need to be made to adapt to the new geographic area.

If you can confidently answer yes to these questions, then it's time to take the next steps in moving toward the next expansion.

To ensure you stay ahead of the challenges of running multiple locations, it's all about the management team. Now follow these steps:

1. **Organize, standardize, and document your operating procedures.**

Nothing about your business operation is too trivial to document. Whether it concerns managing employees, ordering inventory, handling customer complaints, participating in community events, planning menus, or office procedures, you want to codify it all. This information will be helpful for the employees you hire at your new location and those who will keep your current business up and running.

Obviously, certain company secrets should be retained at headquarters. In order to have uniformity of operations and to protect the brand, you will want to have these operating procedures handbooks well distributed to managers and other members of the executive team. When this is a company owned expansion, this is a good idea; when it is a franchise, it is required/mandatory.

Think of it as if you're going to franchise your business and need to create a road map for others to follow detailing how everything works. Essentially, you're systematizing and then writing down details of your company's operations and procedures.

2. **Consult with legal and financial experts to review operational details.**

Opening another business in the same state your business is currently in is less complicated than expanding out of state. However, if that's your plan, it's wise to consult a lawyer to ensure your company name, logo, trademark, and any other intellectual property can be used in the state/s of your new businesses.

Also, if you expand out-of-state, familiarize yourself with the employment laws of that state to ensure you are compliant. Know in advance about any permits or licensing you need for the new state. Make sure the distance to travel from headquarters to the new location is suitable and planned.

In addition, it's smart to check with your attorney and accountant to make sure the current business structure of your company (C Corp, etc.) is the best one for a business with multiple locations. You may want to have a separate legal entity for the new state's locations.

Consult with your insurance agent to see if you can add coverage for the new location/s or if you need separate policies. See if your current company even offers insurance in your new location. You may have to change insurance companies as you expand.

3. **Build your teams.**

While ultimately, you want to consider all your employees as one big team, you are, at first, building two (or more) strong teams of staff and managers. Hopefully, you already have a strong bench of trustworthy and reliable employees whom you can rely on to run the original company since you'll likely spend most of your time at the new business when it first opens.

Ask to see if some of your best employees would transfer to the new location (even if it's just temporarily) so you have a mix of experienced and new workers. Depending on how far apart your locations are, you might need to incentivize them to do this (or at least cover their commuting or inconvenience costs).

Make sure the team running the original location is trained to manage the business as you do and confident enough to make decisions without calling you every ten minutes. In the new place, your current employees should mentor the new hires.

At some point, especially if you plan to expand to multiple locations, you'll want a strong management team in place at each location so you can at the executive level focus on business development and the big picture.

### 4. **Establish a strong communications system with your team.**

As noted, it's essential that your managers are empowered to make decisions. But they also need to know when to check with you when necessary.

While you may be spending most of your time establishing the new business, you should visit your original location at least once or twice a month. Make sure your team knows you're always available by email, text, chat, video conference, instant messaging system, or phone. Consider creating a company intranet to keep all your employees informed.

Hold weekly or bi-weekly meetings with managers and key employees via conference call or video chat. Have your teams submit detailed weekly reports as well. Some POS systems will tell you, at headquarters, minute by minute, hourly, and daily what is going on in each location.

Once you have more than one location, you will develop from within a "new store opening team" where you can stay at headquarters, and the developed team will handle new store openings and evaluations of the manager assigned to the new location.

5. **Promote your company culture and engage your staff with team building activities.**

When your employees are scattered at multiple locations, keeping your team engaged is more challenging. It's important for your entire staff to understand your company culture, vision, and mission and to feel connected—to the business and one another.

Have all-hands-on-deck meetings, online and in-person. It's a good idea to hold company wide fun activities a few times a year. A holiday party, company picnic, or group outing to a ballgame are all excellent team-building activities. Take the time to make staff feel like family.

6. **Invest in tools and technology.**

The right technology simplifies your operations and helps your business function more smoothly. Using cloud based software and apps is critical. Depending on the type of business you own, companies with multiple locations should look for software and apps for:

- POS (point of sale)
- Time-tracking
- Project management
- Inventory management
- Collaboration
- Accounting/payroll
- Productivity suites
- File storage and transfer

- Video conferencing
- Customer Relationship Management (CRM)
- Communication tools
- Payment solutions

Using tools like these saves everyone time, allows for fewer errors, and frees you up for big picture thinking and revenue generating activities.

Train your entire staff to use the technology by holding in-person training sessions or hosting online webinars. If part of your staff works remotely, make sure they have the necessary tools to stay connected, work securely, and get their jobs done. There are many pieces of software and apps to hold and entertain the team together.

7. **Plan for Success**

No matter how successful your business is now, it's imperative that you do your homework when considering expanding to multiple locations. Just because something works in one area doesn't mean it will be equally successful in another.

It takes a lot of preparation to successfully run multiple business locations, whether a store, restaurant, fitness facility, salon, or office. But if you plan carefully, whether you're opening one new location or a dozen, these steps will put you on the right track to success.

# Leadership

Much is spoken about leadership, but what is it?

This is also missing from my college education. The management class is often referred to as company leadership. There was no other mention of leadership in the entire business curriculum.

I have taken many professional continuing education courses, but there are no offerings about leadership. I began working in the early years of management consulting in the C-Suite, and CEOs were paying $25K to take a three-day leadership class.

Over time, I read their course books and began teaching CEOs leadership principles so they could keep their job. There is a saying in the CEO circles that if you keep your job for more than three years, you must be doing something right.

Leadership is the art of inspiring and guiding individuals and groups toward a common vision or goal. It encompasses motivating, influencing, and empowering others to achieve their full potential.

A successful leader exhibits strong interpersonal skills, effective communication, and the capacity to make difficult decisions. They inspire trust and build strong relationships, fostering collaboration and teamwork. Leadership involves setting clear objectives, providing guidance, and nurturing talent.

It requires adaptability, resilience, and the ability to navigate complex situations. Ultimately, leadership is about creating positive change, driving innovation, and leaving a lasting impact on individuals, organizations, and society as a whole.

Leadership is learned behavior. This is something taught in a classroom and role-played in groups or study sessions. Leadership is not passed along genetically, though charisma comes from your uniqueness and is considered genetic. Then, the art is to develop a leadership style with the resources you were given.

Leadership is learned from Universities with CEO programs or coaches that do one-on-one training. The more advanced CEOs meet other CEOs in a mastermind group format.

Those who become leaders are people who believe in themselves and aspire to keep advancing up the organizational ladder. These people have internal fire and know how to call a meeting, organize groups of people, and get them stirred up to move forward as a team to accomplish the new goals, as stated by upper management.

Gaining respect and cooperation are the pearls of good leadership. Then, leaders motivate the group by stating reasons the group should make sure to work in unison to accomplish the goals.

Leaders use their skills, knowledge, and desire to climb to gain respect and cooperation and set the direction for the group's attainment of the goals.

Leaders are all over in an organization. The fire drill leader, assistant manager, manager, first tier manager, all the way up the chain of command to the CEO's desk. If the CEO inspires their lower-tier managers to lead, they, in turn, will inspire their subordinate managers to lead, and this infectious spirit continues down to the rank-and-file employees at the bottom level.

A good leader engages the employees they supervise. A good leader will spread the principles of the company culture, theme, and goal in serving customers and producing high quality products and attention to detail, meeting the company's perfection standard.

Good leadership improves an organization's productivity, execution, precision, and effectiveness. A good leader will understand the needs of the employees, guide and counsel them to enable them to perform well every day. Then, when the goal is accomplished, it is time for celebration and recognition. Having a goal, and using team effort to accomplish the goal, then celebration are cycles that help break up the boredom of coming to work and going home day after day. The feeling of engagement, participation, contribution, and goal attainment is necessary to a workgroup.

Employee training sessions are an absolute necessity today in every industry. These sessions move employees into higher safety awareness, productivity, participation, and joy from the job. Training can be a way to show the employees how to grow within the company. When they feel that they are part of a well-run organization, productivity goes up. When employee sentiment is high, those people tell other people then soon the people they told will apply for a job with the company.

If you are going to start a business and have employees, you will need to exert your leadership skills. This might be frequently represented when you lead training sessions. As the company grows, the training sessions continue in video form but are introduced or concluded by a message from the leader, the top person, the owner, or the company CEO.

The job of CEO pays well, but there is a high turnover in the CEO world. These people struggle every day to do things correctly in accordance with company culture and the direction of the board of directors. The CEO's job is to grow sales and improve earnings. Excuses don't work very well for the CEOs, job performance and execution are everything.

When you begin studying leadership, you learn there are many different prospects of leadership, there are many different approaches to teaching leadership, and quickly, you will learn there is not a common definition of leadership.

Generally speaking, leadership is perceived to be a set of behaviors used by the leader to help a large number of people align their overall direction to focus on and execute prescribed company plans, and leadership is used to continually recharge an organization toward achieving a known set of company goals.

There is an art to being a good leader. Some leaders that are good leaders have natural abilities. Through education and learning, other people learn how to be a good leader.

Leadership is about guiding and impacting outcomes, enabling groups of people to work together to accomplish what they couldn't do working individually.

Leadership's mission is to inspire other people to find energy and enthusiasm and then to join in to accomplish a goal that will put the company in a better position.

**There are certain common behaviors of good leaders:**

- being supportive
- operating with a strong results orientation
- being a good listener
- seeking different perspectives
- surrounding oneself with the smartest and brightest people
- solving problems effectively
- knowing when to bring in outside consultants
- have a clear vision of what your target is

One will quickly learn that leadership is different from management.

When searching for direction, a leader will focus on a specific target by developing a strategy and then translating that strategy into concrete steps. Then, when necessary, they run it by the board of directors who oversee the leader. Then, the appropriate senior managers begin to assign responsibilities to subordinate managers who ensure employees do what they've been assigned, and the plans are adhered to.

The chain of command is a military concept that transfers well into any business model.

Leaders practice empathy, compassion, gratitude, self-awareness, and understanding of any shortcomings. They provide appreciation, gratitude, and support, creating psychological safety and euphoria so their employees are able to collaborate with truth and safety, innovate, and raise issues that are detracting from complete customer satisfaction.

This includes celebrating, acknowledging, and rewarding achievement of the small steps on the way to reaching big goals while enhancing people's well-being, sense of accomplishment, and self-esteem. These conditions have been shown to allow for a team's best performance. Execution and job performance by employees with efficiency is what the leader hopes to achieve.

This performance can be acknowledged and appreciated, while new and continued performance can be energized to be better by giving something to the employee during a team meeting or group gathering. Acknowledgement is a reward for employees. Smaller deeds can be acknowledged from time to time with gift cards of varying sizes. Rewards are part of incenting good performance.

The leader can expand their skills and personality repertoire to create a new level of value for an organization's stakeholders: family members, bankers, investors, private equity firms, and shareholders of company stock.

A discussion of leadership cannot overlook the understanding of charisma. Charisma is the quality of being able to attract, charm, and influence those around you. It is usually easy to identify when someone is charismatic. It is, however, often much harder to say exactly what skills or qualities those people have that other, less charismatic, people lack.

Charismatic people enjoy more career and social success, over and above their skills. They have high emotional intelligence EQ or mental intelligence IQ. As a result, charismatic people earn more, advance faster, make better friends, and are often happier people.

The charismatic person is usually an attractive person with intelligence who knows many things about the industry they work in. They are also good public speakers and can gain the respect and attention of fellow employees while leading groups of people and motivating them to achieve their present goals.

We can learn a lot about charisma from movie actors; in a believable way, some people can convey emotion to get others on board to slay the competition. Some notable people in the CEO world possess a high level of charisma. A bright, attractive, knowledgeable person who lights up a room upon entering and produces noticeable signs that they are a person others will follow.

Other leaders learn how to influence people, lead a group, make people feel comfortable and welcomed, have high energy, and effectively use smiles, getting along well with others.

Leaders mobilize people toward a goal. Leaders create emotional bonds and harmony. Leaders build consensus through participation. Leaders expect excellence with precision.

I have seen many CEOs that have to increase sales. This is why they were hired with the well-established parameters they have been given. They spend their time looking for cash flow statements, meeting with production workers and managers, and meeting with industry organizations and civic groups.

Well, this is all notable, but notice they have not lifted a finger to increase the sales. The direct path is to meet with marketing, order studies of customer satisfaction, improve the product, and move in the direction of creating a product more people will want.

Then, use marketing to deliver the message to a targeted group of known users of the product. With the day-to-day demands of your job, you can lose direction and forget to do those essential steps of inviting more people to enjoy your product.

Leadership has to know the course and stay on course to reach the target. This would be the CEO and other members of senior management.

Leadership is a skill that must be taught, learned, and developed over time through training, practice, and repetition. Some people are born with attributes that enable them to develop faster and outperform others as they develop their leadership skills.

Leaders provide guidance, inspiration, and motivation when achieving goals. They create a vision and develop goals, then rally people around the common cause of reaching well defined goals. Leaders possess the necessary skills and knowledge to make informed decisions and solve problems effectively. Leaders collaborate and take in information from as many sources they have access to, digest the information, and then are tasked with making the final decision.

Leadership can be difficult. You have to work with a range of personalities, raise motivations, provide mentorship, continue learning, and meet the goals dictated to you, all at the same time. On top of all that, the environment inside and outside your company is constantly shifting.

The most common reason leaders fail is that they don't communicate their vision effectively to their team. Mostly, this is the case because they don't have a vision. Failure to lead can result from several factors, including a lack of clarity about the target, indecisiveness, and lack of confidence. They have not brought the employee base on board to pursue the goal. Daily, they are doing other work steps, staying busy, and are not focused on the number one issue, such as raising the sales numbers, controlling the costs, and delivering to the stakeholders' higher earnings, consistent with higher returns on investment.

While coaching CEOs, we point out that leadership skills are learned; you have to spend time practicing the skills. Just being in the role of a leader is insufficient; you have to set goals, participate in designed learning experiences, ask for feedback, and get coaching. You also have to put in the time every day and make learning leadership a daily habit. It is critical for leaders to be positive, energetic, and hopeful while guiding others.

CEOs and mostly boards of directors hire management consultants to visit with the CEO and make sure the tasks they are performing on a daily basis are leading toward the desired results. Management consultants can do studies to measure customer satisfaction and bring these results back to the CEO. Management consultants can keep the CEO armed with information, focused on solving the main problem and delegating other tasks to subordinates to clear the CEO's desk to take immediate steps to raise sales, improve the product, control the costs, and deliver record setting earnings.

At first, CEOs perceive management consultants as a threat, but over time, CEOs become reliant on management consultants to keep them on task to perform important steps. CEOs will learn that management consultants do these same steps over and over again on a daily basis and are honed in the skill of taking the steps to improve sales and deliver record setting earnings.

Most venture capital and private equity firms will not release the money until the management consultants are named, contracted with, and engaged by the company to keep the leader of the company focused on the task of improving sales, controlling costs, and delivering as close as possible positive earnings while growing the company.

Leadership and boards of directors know that growth poised companies are using funds to improve infrastructure, train and develop teams, purchase inventory, and do things to poise the company for future positive earnings.

Most strong growth oriented companies are not producing present day profits. Management consultants are there to get people on track and focus on company growth without wasting resources or expanding in the wrong direction, such as broadening the fleet of company owned jets.

Operating a growth company takes a special talent. This is not a level company with day-in and day-out static duties. This is like managing a rocket that just took off from a spaceport. You want to hang on for dear life and make good decisions that adhere to the organized plan established in the beginning.

The key to getting a growth company under control is attracting and expanding the customer base so that these new sales will pay for continued growth. Then, eventually, the company will level out where day-to-day management becomes more static.

Operating a growth company is one of my favorite consulting projects. I help management and company leaders who are experienced and up for the challenges. Challenges that come with speed to you every day.

In some entrepreneurial study groups of self-employed individuals, the studies find that leaders of small businesses are known to spend too much time on the technical skill of the business and not enough time on the management of the business or its marketing efforts.

They often fail to read the financial statements produced by the accounting team. They lead the business whimsically and follow an internal native guide of finishing the present job without much thought of filling the company pipeline with jobs for the next 18 months.

They don't spend much time with innovation or considering new lines of work that could contribute to the growth and expansion of the business. They spend no time looking for businesses to purchase that would expand their customer base, bringing profits and the owner's salary to new heights.

Actual day-to-day tasks and responsibilities of an organizational leader include managing and motivating a team utilizing a problem solving mindset to address any conflicts or problems that may arise or threaten a business. They spend time setting team goals and coordinating with other departments as broader organizational goals are pursued.

Bringing children into the management and leadership of a medium-sized business can be a difficult task. One has to be there to help the new executive gain acceptance by the employee base. The new executive needs to be given tasks that they can perform well. Slow steps need to be taken to introduce the new executive to the group. Usually, the new executive comes from a strong educational background or may possess MBA credentials, which, when presented, might make it believable that this new 28-year-old executive might know something.

Learning leadership skills enhances your feelings of self-worth, meaningfulness, contribution, and accomplishment. The greater your skills, the more comfortable and confident you will become. When you exude confidence, others will gladly follow.

**CHAPTER 9**

# The Psychology of a Business Owner

One has to be aware of the field of psychology when becoming a business owner. The business owner cannot put their head in the sand, only perform steps they know then hope that some more sales will come to the cash register.

Not all people are cut out for self-employment. Generally, you have to be someone who is in touch with their core values and beliefs, and they have to be someone who wants to be successful and achieve something. Your belief structure has to be in the right place for you to give permission to yourself to accept this challenge and start a business of your own.

Tough love from a psychiatrist can be a powerful and effective approach to help individuals enter the business of entrepreneurship. It involves providing strong, straightforward, and sometimes challenging feedback to motivate and support entrepreneurs in overcoming their fears and other mental barriers and moving toward accepting the challenge and agreeing on becoming successful.

Here's a more in-depth explanation of how tough love from a psychiatrist can be beneficial in the context of entrepreneurship.

Entrepreneurs often carry limiting beliefs about themselves and their abilities. These beliefs can stem from past experiences, upbringing, or societal conditioning. A psychiatrist employing tough love will challenge these beliefs and encourage the entrepreneur to question and reframe them. By dismantling self-limiting beliefs, the entrepreneur becomes more open to possibilities and can envision success in new ways.

Fear of failure, fear of judgment, fear of the unknown – these are common challenges that entrepreneurs face. A psychiatrist using tough love will push the entrepreneur to confront these fears head-on. Instead of avoiding difficult situations, tough love helps entrepreneurs embrace their fears as part of the entrepreneurial journey. This can lead to increased resilience and a willingness to take calculated risks.

Entrepreneurship is filled with uncertainty, and often, entrepreneurs encounter situations they've never experienced before. Tough love from a psychiatrist emphasizes embracing challenges rather than shying away from them. Entrepreneurs are encouraged to view challenges as opportunities for growth and learning. This mindset shift enables them to tackle new situations with confidence, adaptability, and a problem solving mindset.

Entrepreneurship is all about venturing into uncharted territories. It requires stepping outside one's comfort zone and navigating through ambiguity. A psychiatrist providing tough love will push entrepreneurs to face the unknown and embrace ambiguity without letting it paralyze them. This mindset fosters a greater sense of curiosity, innovation, and a willingness to experiment.

Tough love involves holding entrepreneurs accountable for their actions and decisions. A psychiatrist will challenge them to take ownership of their choices and outcomes. This accountability fosters a sense of responsibility, discipline, and commitment to achieving their goals, even when the going gets tough.

Entrepreneurship is a rollercoaster ride filled with ups and downs. Tough love helps entrepreneurs develop emotional resilience by encouraging them to face setbacks and failures with a positive attitude. Resilience allows entrepreneurs to bounce back from adversity, learn from their experiences, and keep moving forward.

Growth often occurs when individuals step outside their comfort zones. A psychiatrist employing tough love will push entrepreneurs to break free from complacency and strive for continuous improvement. This might involve taking on new challenges, seeking mentorship, or seeking feedback from peers and customers.

Tough love from a psychiatrist in the context of entrepreneurship aims to break down mental barriers, foster resilience, and push individuals to reach their full potential. It's about encouraging entrepreneurs to face their fears, embrace uncertainty, and challenge themselves in ways that lead to personal and professional growth. This approach can be transformative for entrepreneurs, helping them build the mindset and skills necessary to thrive in the world of business.

You have to do your own inner work with the help of an entrepreneurship oriented psychologist or psychiatrist. Many start-up entrepreneurs dive into the water and swim like a fish. It's for the people who are afraid to give it a try; they have to enter with the proper support and in the right mental state.

Then, when you begin doing well, you cannot be afraid of success.

Success can demand more time, energy, and commitment, potentially leading to a fear of losing work-life balance. Entrepreneurs might worry that their personal lives, relationships, or well-being will suffer as they dedicate themselves to their growing ventures.

Success can attract attention from others, and entrepreneurs may fear the added pressure and expectations from society, colleagues, employees, and even family and friends. This pressure can feel overwhelming and may lead to anxiety about living up to others' expectations.

Success can trigger jealousy or envy in others, and entrepreneurs might fear the negative consequences of standing out or becoming more prosperous than their peers. This fear could lead to feelings of isolation or a reluctance to share their achievements openly. Many entrepreneurs are new at being number one. They have to grow into this, be proud of their achievements, and be courteous and graceful. Some could suffer from grown Egos, and this behavior is not pleasing to others.

With greater success often comes increased responsibility and accountability. Entrepreneurs may worry about the impact of their decisions on their employees, customers, and stakeholders, and the fear of making mistakes or poor choices can be a significant source of stress.

Success may challenge an entrepreneur's self-worth and identity. If they tie their self-esteem primarily to their business achievements, they may fear that failure in their venture could imply personal inadequacy.

Past experiences with success and trying to achieve success can also influence an entrepreneur's current attitude. They may be apprehensive about repeating the same patterns if they have encountered negative outcomes after previous successes. This time, they can do it with gracefulness and courtesy toward others.

It is important to note that not all entrepreneurs experience a fear of success, and the intensity of this fear can vary significantly among individuals. Addressing and overcoming these fears often involves self-reflection, setting realistic expectations, seeking support from peers or mentors, and, if necessary, seeking professional guidance from psychologists or therapists to develop coping strategies and build resilience. Then, work on strategies to embrace success and have a hunger to achieve more and greater success.

All of this can be as simple as opening a donut shop. Operating the donut shop for ten years in one location. Then, after taking a few courses and reading some books, the entrepreneur gets the financing and opens three more stores. One year later, six more stores, now with ten stores, the profits are much bigger than before, one has to enjoy, savor, and like this position. Then, become ready to open 30 more stores.

You have to be ambitious, driven to succeed, competitive, and able to learn new things. To grow your business, learning new things is a constant. Ambition is defined as having or showing a strong desire and determination to succeed. An ambitious person is someone who is always striving to reach a goal. Through hard work, dedication, and perseverance, an ambitious person doesn't give up. They push forward and are determined to succeed.

You may have learned to accept a leadership role in your company. You may have to learn what your employee's needs are. The answers to all of these questions and concerns are addressed in the field of psychology.

You have to be willing to start a business and then learn more about yourself. Do you have a desire to achieve, and can you say the word success without throwing up? Many people, through self-sabotage, do things that prevent themselves from being successful. You have to be willing to rise up and take your company to the top.

People who are clear about their beliefs and core values have the strongest chance of achieving success.

Success includes being a decent person with high moral values and must demonstrate they have good character and integrity.

Can you imagine sitting in a room with a football player or a new musician who just had the number-one-selling album? You tell them they have met with success, and in order to have more success, they have to adopt a life with high morals and values and must demonstrate good character and integrity daily. If you don't do this, you will never be chosen to hold up a Cheerios box and make more money from the endorsements, which will pay them more money than they can ever earn as an athletic player or musician. Yes, psychology plays a role.

The business owner has to have a good example lifestyle in order to protect the brand of the company. The business owner needs to treat employees, vendors, and customers with high integrity. Everyone in business needs a little psychology to brush up from the neck up to reach success.

True success rests with the numbers. Did you reach for the stars and attain close to what you intended to? Did you become another overachiever who underachieved? You do not want to become the high achiever who achieved the lowest sales results.

What achievement is can be argued, but the blunt truth is that it is in the sales. Did your company achieve $100 million in sales?

There is a formula and road to follow to get every business in America to $100 million in sales. You need to learn and become informed about the formula. Get yourself onto the road to high achievement.

Don't stand by. Go through the motions and become the lowest performing overachiever in business, a title you would not want to have the trophy for.

Success has to be studied, and your relationship with success has to become known by your psychology professional.

The Merriam-Webster Dictionary says success is a favorable or desired outcome. Also, the attainment of wealth, favor, or eminence. One that succeeds.

Dictoionay.com says success is: noun. The favorable or prosperous termination of attempts or endeavors; the accomplishment of one's goals. The attainment of wealth, position, honors, or the like. A performance or achievement marked by success, as by the attainment of honors.

The fear of success often stems from the pressure to meet higher expectations, a fear of change, the unknown—I am not worthy syndrome and the potential for increased responsibilities. It can also be linked to self-doubt, fear of losing personal connections, and the perception of success altering one's identity and lifestyle.

## Other made-public definitions of success are:

Success is: the result of perfection, hard work, learning from failure, loyalty, and persistence.

Success is: It could mean a sense of accomplishment and career progression. It could mean being able to do the things you love. It could mean being able to provide the best possible upbringing for your children.

- Set powerful goals
- Give your brain a place to aim
- Focus with a positive attitude

- Build high self-esteem
- Believe in yourself, have confidence
- Take pride in what you do
- Research/learning/action/scaling
- Success is achievement-focused
- Success provides confidence, security, a sense of well-being, the ability to contribute at a greater level
- If you want to be successful, you need to have a clear goal and a growth mindset.
- Success in business is the attainment of a goal with the receipt of a financial reward.
- Keep your eye on the prize. There is the $100 million goal and the $500 million goal, or the $800 million goal, when measured by sales.

In getting ready to learn more about psychology and how it applies to having a successful self-employed business activity, let's look at a personal achievement inventory. In dealing with people who own their own business, many different parts of the organization and the many parts of the owner need attention.

Here is a list to savor as we require business owners to be in touch with these keywords: so, test yourself. Write the word on a sheet of paper the write you present day definition of the word.

| | | |
|---|---|---|
| accomplishment | economy | organize |
| ambition | engage | performance |
| ask for help | execute | persevere |
| collaborate | financial gain | plan |
| commitment | focused | prosperity |
| committed | fulfilling | realization |
| competitive | good habits | responsibility |
| creative | grow | strive |
| determined | guide/lead/train | thriving |
| driven | Involved | tolerant |
| economic aim | learn to learn | victory |
| endure stress | motivated | wealth |
| | net worth building | winning |
| | networking | work hard |
| | | work smart |

When the business owner has on hand and top of mind an understanding and definition of these keywords, they become better informed about the requirements and responsibilities of owning a business.

Some people wince at the financial reference to success. Some people are not in favor of other people who want to achieve success.

I have heard it from a room full of unsuccessful people who want to argue with you about what success is. Some advice is: don't listen to them. Get onto the road for success and climb the mountain as fast as you can to attain success for you, your business, and your family.

Psychology is the scientific study of the mind and behavior. Psychologists actively study and understand mental processes, brain functions, and behavior.

Psychology plays a part in starting a business. Starting a business is like riding a camel; you don't know where it's going to go and when it wants to stop for water. Some people liken starting a business to riding a unicycle. You try to move forward, but you have to learn how to keep your balance, because there are multiple (360) ways you can fall off the unicycle!

The most challenging part of being an entrepreneur is getting on the camel. I meet so many people who tell me about their business ideas and all their plans to become an entrepreneur, but few of these people possess the courage to begin the process. I'm not telling you that it will be smooth sailing from here on in, but I am telling you that the first step is the hardest part.

It is important to know that mentors can help. Mentors have literally saved some people many years' worth of mistakes. If you don't know, you cannot grow, and sometimes, in order to know, you have to learn. Learning from others who have already experienced what you are contending with can be quite helpful and valuable. You don't have to be a pioneer. Reach out for help along the way.

Understanding psychological principles can help you in every aspect of growing your business, from marketing and selling to leadership to know when your ego is getting in the way of progress. Psychology is helpful in guiding you on how to deal with your employees. Every entrepreneur should gain a working knowledge of psychology if they want to take their companies and themselves to the next level.

Knowledge of entrepreneurship psychology helps answer some vital questions in business, such as who your customers are, what they are like, and what makes them choose your service. Knowing the answers to these questions often leads to successful marketing campaigns in aware companies.

Of course, not all types of entrepreneurs share the same psychological makeup.

The traits behind the psychology of entrepreneurship may depend on each person's experience, background, education, vision, and goals. However, some qualities may be more valuable than others in helping entrepreneurs succeed. If you are an entrepreneur or an aspiring entrepreneur, understanding how psychology plays a role in determining business success can be critical.

Available to aspiring entrepreneurs is the entire industry of self-help. There have been created and still being contemplated are tapes, YouTube videos, books, e-books, and other mediums to get you self-help information to help you feel better about yourself. Information will help you understand the mechanics of closing a sale, making a cold call, establishing a network, and negotiating. There is an abundance of knowledge out there.

One cannot go too far into modern day self-help without discovering the work of Tony Robbins. There are some who love Tony and the work that he did. Not to be overlooked is the work he did in spreading the word about the techniques of NLP. Neuro-linguistic programming (NLP) understanding can help everyone who has any kind of relationship with another human being on earth.

The idea is that you can connect better with someone if you know how they like to receive input. Some people are visual, some are auditory, and some are kinesthetic. This information can help business relationships, marriage relationships, dating relationships, and all other relationships. This information can help you, and it is valuable to know.

Every person is unique. It's not that we are born and that one sister, sister number three, is the entrepreneur. We all function in a different way. Some people go through life as heavily left brained and marry someone right brained; both have an emotional intelligence level of 7, and it is balance they seek. They may have good communication skills, but one is very, extremely detailed in explanation. The other is more happy-go-lucky and may forget the details from time to time.

The entrepreneur needs to be studied. They broke out of the mold, and the indications are they are ambitious and able to assume some level of risk for the purpose of getting to a better place in life. The entrepreneur is not, by definition, an innovator. Innovation in entrepreneurship is helpful but not required. On average, of most people who start a business of their own, 85% of them are not innovators.

Enthusiasm is helpful, and the right brained person would likely be the source of enthusiasm. These people can enthusiastically mop the floor, do the dishes, fold the laundry, and then light up a customer who comes through the door with charm and wit.

There is no one personality type that is going to be the business owner. Certain personality types are better suited to be an owner. From the psychologist's point of view, they observe… that here is a person that is in business for themselves. What have we got? We can begin to understand what we have through interviews and some simple tests.

If we have someone who is right brained, we have to alert the business to look out for the details, as this person is not going to care about the details and not spend much time on record keeping. Most likely, it will be suitable to let them mix with the customers and explain how the business can be of assistance to them. These people are often found in marketing or sales and come to work with a smile and cheerfulness that can be contagious.

The left brained person is not going to charm the customers. In fact, it might be better to keep them away from the customers, except on the rare occasion the customer wants to know how the component parts of their Swiss watch all work together to keep perfect time.

Then, at this time, let the left brained person communicate with the customers. The left brained person in accounting or engineering is a unique bird and very helpful to the business enterprise. This person likes technical details and has a good sense of order and organization. They will keep their space clean, and the product is manufactured in accordance with specifications. Their keen sense of detail will make sure that everything is done in the right order in the right way, and shooting for perfection comes naturally to them.

When hiring employees, be sure not to hire a salon worker or salesperson to run your accounting department. Do not let someone with a long history in accounting run your marketing function or customer relations.

The point is there is balance. There are people who have a high emotional EQ, a medium intellectual IQ, and are well balanced with some right-brained skills and some left-brained skills. They can live in one environment and quite easily switch to the other when necessary.

In this example, this person is the ideal candidate who will be successful in owning their own business. There are many, many variations of this profile.

Psychologists say it is a person's personality and characteristics that motivate them to be an entrepreneur. From this viewpoint, entrepreneurs are born with the innate capability to be successful because of who they are, personally motivated and driven by a need for achievement.

By persisting in entrepreneurial behavior, relentlessly pursuing established goals, and investing a lot of time and energy, entrepreneurs can achieve successful entrepreneurship and obtain the desired goal of economic benefits.

Some offer that entrepreneurs possess a need for achievement, which drives their activity and their ability to achieve success. Entrepreneurs display and utilize a distinctive thought process called effectual thinking, which is based on creativity.

The psychology of entrepreneurship relates to understanding the relationship between successful business leadership and the mental techniques and characteristics that thriving entrepreneurs possess.

Successful entrepreneurs tend to be reasonably self-confident, more risk-averse than you might think, and extremely passionate about their ideas.

You can overcome your fear of success, failure, uncertainty, and anxiety by surrounding yourself with positive people.

There is a diversity of approaches to personality testing and assessment. Controversy surrounds many aspects of the widely used methods and techniques. These include such assessments as interviews, rating scales, self-reports, personality inventories, projective techniques, and behavioral observation.

Some will say entrepreneurship is the process of identifying and developing economic and social opportunities through the efforts of individuals and organizations. This can result in starting and building new businesses in pursuit of profit, either as independent enterprises or within incumbent organizations.

Motivation, focus, goal clarity, resilience, and stress management are all mental demands on anyone striving to be the best in their field. Here are four core mental skills of successful entrepreneurs known the world over that you must master if you desire to be a successful entrepreneurial business leader.

1. **Set the focus of your goals high.**

If you were to set a sales goal of $850,000, would you schedule an activity that might only bring you and your team that amount? Or would you set your team's sights on reaching $900,000? The technique here is to set your main goals at a point beyond the ones that are your baseline. The goal you are given becomes a goal you'll reach along the way. With high focus comes high achievement when the whole team participates in unison together

2. **Visualization skills will accelerate your progress.**

From champion athletes, we know that visualization works and is helpful in becoming successful. Visualization can help you reach your goals more quickly and with greater accuracy.

In visualization for golfers, they are instructed the night before to locate 18 sheets of blank white paper. On the paper, they draw or sketch each hole on the scorecard, and the sheets are numbered 1 through 18.

Draw the tee box and where your first shot lands. Then draw where your second shot lands, and then draw where your next shot lands. This exercise is designed to contain three holes on the front nine and three holes on the back nine that will be one under par, or the target is to score a "birdie."

Then, the conclusion of the exercise is to sit in a chair, close your eyes, hold each sheet of paper in your dominant hand, and now, with your eyes closed, visualize each shot you are going to take on this hole. See the ball leave the club, go high in the air, and land in your target zone. Keep your eyes closed, pause, then visualize the next more critical and precise shot and see it land 18 inches from the hole, using the slope of the green to get the ball to stop within 18 inches from the flagstick. See the ball leave the club, see the ball in the air, see the ball land and roll to the hole.

This goes on for each of the 18 holes. You can see the exercise is to let the mind build a sketch of what is supposed to happen tomorrow when you physically go to the golf course. Then, at the end of the day, see how well you did in putting down on the course what you visualized in the drill the night before.

It's the same in business; you can visualize how your sales will go up, how controlling costs will make the overall costs go down, and a big visual of how profit/earnings will go up as a result of your efforts.

We can use visualization in business for small tasks or big tasks. The idea is to get a clear picture in your mind of what you set out to do. Then, when you physically go to the office, be sure you are taking the steps to get you to where you want to be at the end of the month.

Effective visualization and imagery need to be planned, sequenced, and honed. The reticular activating system (RAS) in your brain stem filters information that supports and guides you to achieve what you focus on. You, therefore, want to be careful about what dominates your mind's eye.

Your aim is to create visualization and vivid imagery of the results and achievements you want to achieve. Eyes closed, you want to create movement and animation. Sequence the snapshots to roll like a movie scene, the same way you experience while dreaming.

Incorporate all your senses, and make your visualizations as real as possible. Include in your visualizations smell, taste, touch, weather, and sound details. When you do, you activate and better train the neurocircuitry that will pivot your thinking, behavior, and attention in the direction of the business goals you desire.

Practice regularly, preferably daily. A Harvard Medical School psychiatrist explains the profound benefits of undertaking deliberate sessions of positive, constructive daydreams. The working memory processes in your brain can solve problems better and generate ideas you cannot normally access in pressured situations. This moves you into a state of creativity.

3. **Practice introspective reflection for greater resilience.**

As business leaders, we endure many more highly stress inducing situations and encounters than our subordinates. Stress and conflict you will encounter frequently when owning your own business. Here are some steps for relief and recovery.

Pause regularly, quiet introspection, meditate by slowing down for twelve minutes, then return to work. Pausing your thought process increases your attention span and reduces feelings of anxiety. This will reduce the effect of negative or critical dialog toward others.

Become an observer of your emotions, and consider the good feelings when you mentally and emotionally unravel. When you are feeling frustrated, angry, or overwhelmed? Be aware of your feelings and use quiet introspection to relax your entire body, mind, and feelings.

Reduce your negative self-talk and boost your system so you are back to a positive state.

When you step into self-observation, you instantly engage your left brain's analytical skills. From this switch, the intensity of your right brained activity, which is emotional expression, will drop. Your mind's capacity has more freedom to think clearly and rationally.

As you become a master of introspection and self-awareness, you will find those stress triggers will no longer affect you as severely. They will no longer control you as you have paused to develop the power to manage them.

4. **Practice positivity and optimism through reframing while also acknowledging the negatives.**

Customers say things that are hurtful to manipulate you to lower the bill. This causes you to recoil as you sense conflict. Reframing will allow you to see this is only a ruse by the customer to get their way. It is not a bad reflection on your product or service.

Business entrepreneurs, by definition, usually choose a way of thinking which the team they lead does not. Your job is to tread where others fear in pursuit of progress, growth, and business success. Risk mitigation can turn into challenges, creating emotional and mental turmoil that could fracture us and our employees. Guilt, denial, and shame are common by products in the business leader's daily life.

The instant you permit yourself to acknowledge the negatives, like a mistake or failure, you draw a close to any prolonged mental turmoil you've been experiencing. From the point of confessing: "It is my fault, I goofed up, and the impact has been disastrous," the only way you can go from here is up. This is an important part of the process.

Practice optimism to then take yourself and your team forward by debriefing the group in a team meeting as they provide answers to the following questions:

- What happened today?
- What went wrong?
- What are the positives we can draw from this?
- What are the lessons gained from this?
- What policy or procedure change can be made to avoid the same outcome occurring?

- What perspectives and ideas have arisen out of this undesirable outcome?

Successful leaders always hunt for answers to these questions. Your search for these answers restores your (and your employees') growth mindset. Ideas and possibilities will start to turn the wheels toward productivity again. Regained momentum will have you and your team looking and going forward again in no time.

There are four character traits that most entrepreneurs possess: Vision, passion, adaptability, and resilience.

1. **Vision:** To see the future and direct the company to hit the targeted sales!

2. **Passion:** All entrepreneurs do self-employment because of the passion, that inner feeling of joy, to do what they do.

3. **Adaptability:** Agile on your feet, pivots quickly to make your product or service more useful and accessible in the marketplace.

4. **Resilience:** The ability to hang in there regardless of the opposing force and see to it the job is done right.

We have to have a way to cope and deal with the day's events. We cannot just ignore what happened with great hope it will not happen again. We have to use our skills to address, acknowledge, and recover from things that go against the grain or disrupt our day. We are learning that introspection, meditation, acknowledgment, positivity, and remedy are the ways to get things back to normal again, poised for higher productivity and sales.

We also need to do a self-check to see that life consists of continuous learning. Your job is not done until your sales are over $800,000,000. That is the black-and-white of entrepreneurship. If your sales are short, so is your learning. Learn more and do more to convert your job into an executive position. Continue to grow until you have reached not your desired level but achieve a benchmark equal to the very top ten in your industry. It is the pursuit of achievement that is the juice that keeps entrepreneurs motivated and interested.

**CHAPTER 10**

# Change is Constant

Just like the weather on a ship, change is constant. Managing a business is similar. Weather is constantly changing at sea on the ship. Therefore, the ship's crew has to make the necessary changes and adjustments as directed by the captain of the ship.

Every day in business is different. Different issues, different challenges, and the persistent need to increase sales and keep customers happy. If you are on top of your business, you will see when the team of employees will have to make the necessary changes and adjustments as directed by the owner of the business.

Making changes and adjustments, keeping up with the challenges before you, and new things affecting your business are necessary. When you are on top of your game, you will see clearly the changes, and then you will know what to adjust. When reacting to changes, you have to remain focused on the target, the goal for the end of the quarter.

When you are asleep at the wheel, you will feel like every day is the same as yesterday. Eventually, you will wake up because something bit you on the backside on both cheeks.

Embracing change is important. Keeping up with technology is important because technology may be on the verge of making your business extinct. Stay on top of the issues, embrace change, and resolve conflicts. You have to reserve time to do this to be the captain of the ship.

Embracing change is a very important part of running a business. In the 1950s through 1970s, doing the same thing the same way and trying to make the process more perfect was much the trend in business operations.

Then, the year 2000 came with social behavior change, technology bursting at the seams, and coming into the marketplace. There were conventions being held conditioning people about change. There were seminars to tell you how to cope with change.

The whole circuit of corporate speakers was available to tell you about change, how to expect it, and how to deal with it. Now, years later, in the 21st century, change is obvious, and it is a constant in running a business.

New tax law, employment law, processes, procedures, software, shipping policies, economic policies, and a new app. There are a lot of new things that could be adopted for your business to help it run better.

Change and the theories of change disrupted the marketplace. Still, in the early 2000s, CEOs lost their jobs because they came in and tried to steer the company toward new methods and procedures. The workers and managers wanted a CEO to come aboard and do things the same way as last year and the year before. Most of these notions met with the board of directors' approval.

Then, when sales did not go up, and overall earnings went down, the CEO was to blame and then got fired. Change in an organization has to come methodically and over time when all the workers and managers understand the need for change, embrace it, and become part of the process of change.

Smaller companies don't have these problems because the owner, on any given day, can say, "Hold it, we are going to make some changes here. Now listen to me while I tell you what those changes are going to be."

Since the year 2000, so much has changed, and change is now ordinary. New apps, software, hardware, and tools to make the job easier have been developed. CEOs are becoming hired because their reputation is that of being a disruptor. Throw out the old. In with the new.

The modern CEO says: "Out with the old, in comes the new. Step aside now. I've got work to do. Clearing the path, there's no delay. I'll reshape your day. Heads up for what may come your way!"

The marketing function is trying to partner in order to get in front of new market conditions that could bring new customers to purchase the company's products or services. Partnering is fashionable today. Partnering through your network is the trend. Reaching beyond your network is a coveted skill.

The everyday life of the small and medium-sized business entrepreneur is to get up with fresh ideas on how to drive sales, then balance the company with a production force that could keep pace with new sales orders that were recently committed to.

Today, companies of all types and sizes initiate change for good, solid reasons. From the C-Suite to the front lines, people and teams figure out new ways to solve customer problems, improve products, expand the product line, create new revenue streams, and reduce costs. This is the CEO's template for change.

The company leaders need to spot opportunities for change, gather, and determine a plan of implementation. Then, announce to the employees here is what we are going to do, this is how we are going to do it, what is it going to look like, what is its purpose. Then, bring the employees around as informed souls informed and ready to assist with implementing the change. The company's introduction of change is important, then gathering the support from all the employees.

Upper management has the responsibility to provide the necessary tools and resources to help implement the desired change. When change is scheduled, there may be some unexpected costs along the way. This has to become part of the budgetary calculation and be provided on time to make the change process fluid and uninterrupted.

Change needs to be monitored and measured to make sure the change leads to improvement, which means increased; sales and customer satisfaction.

Due to the rapid pace of change in companies today, demand for people who can implement and lead successful change ideas far outstrips the supply. Beware of resumes that highlight change agents or disruptors. They may be telling themselves about their bad behavior and inability to work as a team or team leader. You want to be thorough in your due diligence regarding hiring practices of people who can truly lead and implement in the direction of change without rocking the boat.

From a CEO's perspective in a medium-sized private company, being alert to change is crucial for the success of the company for several reasons.

In today's dynamic business environment, change is constant. Staying alert and responsive to change enables a company to identify emerging trends, technological advancements, and market shifts before competitors. By adapting quickly, the company can gain a competitive advantage by offering innovative products or services that meet the evolving needs of customers.

Change often stems from changing customer preferences, expectations, and demands. By being alert to these changes, a company can proactively adjust its strategies, processes, and offerings to meet customer requirements. This customer centric approach enhances customer satisfaction and loyalty, leading to increased sales and market share.

Change often brings new market opportunities that can be leveraged to expand the company's business. By monitoring industry trends, customer behavior, and emerging markets, the CEO can identify untapped segments or niches and capitalize on them. Being alert to change allows the company to seize opportunities and grow its revenue streams.

Change also brings risks, such as unwanted disruptive technologies, regulatory changes from many directions, regulatory compliance issues that may not be current with the times, or economic fluctuations. By being alert to these potential risks, the CEO can develop proactive strategies to mitigate their impact. This may involve diversifying revenue streams, adopting agile decision making processes, obtaining regulatory permission, investing in research and development, or hiring consulting firms to stay ahead of industry disruptions.

Being alert to change fosters a culture of adaptability and agility within the organization. This mindset encourages employees to embrace change, be open to new ideas, and continuously improve processes. An agile company can respond swiftly to market shifts, reposition itself, and make informed decisions, enhancing its ability to navigate uncertainties successfully.

Change often fuels innovation and growth. The CEO can identify opportunities for product or service enhancements, process improvements, or business model innovations by staying alert. Embracing change encourages a culture of innovation and implementation, with precision execution, allowing the company to stay ahead of the curve and drive sustainable growth.

Anticipating and adapting to change prepares the company for the future. By closely monitoring industry trends, technological advancements, and societal shifts, the CEO can ensure the company remains relevant and resilient in the long term. This proactive approach helps the company to withstand disruptions, maintain its market position, and capitalize on future opportunities.

Being alert to change is vital for a medium-sized private company's success, as it enables the CEO to identify and seize opportunities, mitigate risks, enhance customer satisfaction, foster innovation, and drive growth. By embracing change, the company can position itself as a dynamic and adaptive organization in today's fast paced business landscape. Designing and leading a company that is agile, dynamic, adaptive, and welcomes change to get ahead is the desired approach for today's markets.

The purpose of this book is to look forward and see what true entrepreneurship is all about today. It would be good to take a look back occasionally and study the antics of one of the large acquirers of businesses, 3G Capital, a private equity firm. These people buy, invest in companies, and implement rapid and immediate change. They are organized and trained for this purpose. Their tactics are on the edge of ruthless in the immediate way they make a change to a mature and ongoing company.

3G Capital is a global investment firm and a private partnership built on an owner-operator approach to investing in substantial companies over a long-term horizon. Founded in 2004, the firm is best known for its long-term investments in Anheuser Busch, Burger King, and Kraft Heinz.

The firm is best known for implementing zero based budgeting, which is a budgeting technique that all government agencies should adopt. It means you get zero budget for the year unless you can prove with documentation that the funds are needed to drive the company efficiently.

The 3G machine has two main profit drivers. First, there is the tried and true merger play of becoming more profitable through consolidation and expansion into new markets. Then, the second profit driver is the sharp pencils come out, and the combined company creates value by cutting costs dramatically down to the number of times per month the water in the water cooler should be changed.

The Kraft deal cemented the position of 3G as the leading change agent in the food and beverage business. 3G Capital management has a style. It might be too drastic for the taste of most professional management teams, but it is drastic, and it has proven to be effective over and over again.

In every organization, change is possible regardless of how drastic the needed change may be or how much resistance current management throws up. Many companies are in need of change, but it is current management that is blocking the way for change. Many times, change is needed immediately to keep pace and in touch with the times.

As consultants, we often see management say we can't do this, we can't do that, as their company is quickly sinking. Some companies need to change immediately to refresh and keep up with the demands of the consumer. When the style of consumer demand changes, your company must make immediate changes to keep existing customers happy. Then you outmaneuver slow to change companies or competitors; thus, by making immediate change, your company becomes more attractive to consumer demands, you keep happy existing business and capture new business.

Here listed are only a few of the companies that failed to keep up with the trends and innovate to offer their customers something new: Blockbuster, Polaroid, Toys R US, Tower Records, Kodak, Kmart, Nokia, Bed Bath & Beyond, and Sears.

It is not necessary to have in your organization a 'department of change,' but times may continue to change, thus requiring such a functioning department to keep your vision of the future on track to appeal to consumer demand. This department would be constantly scanning the waters ahead to provide directional changes and feedback to keep the company on track for delivering effective modern day customer satisfaction. In business today, this is a function of the innovation department within a company.

In today's dynamic and fast paced business environment, change has become a constant and vital aspect of staying competitive and relevant. The rapid advancement of technology, globalization, shifting market trends, and evolving customer expectations have significantly altered the way businesses operate.

The business landscape is constantly evolving, and organizations must adapt to survive and thrive. Failure to embrace change can lead to obsolescence and loss of market share. By staying responsive and agile, businesses can seize new opportunities, address emerging challenges, and capitalize on evolving market and technology trends.

Change often drives innovation and fosters growth. By encouraging a culture of change, businesses can explore new ideas, develop creative solutions, and bring innovative products or services to market. Embracing change enables organizations to stay ahead of competitors and maintain their relevance in an ever changing marketplace.

Customers are the lifeblood of any business, and their needs and demands constantly evolve. By keeping a close eye on customer demand, businesses can proactively anticipate their preferences, expectations, and pain points. This allows organizations to tailor their offerings, improve customer experiences, and deliver superior value, thus building customer loyalty and driving long term success.

Change provides opportunities for organizations to gain a competitive edge. By embracing change and adapting quickly, businesses can differentiate themselves from competitors. This may involve adopting new technologies, improving operational efficiencies, or implementing disruptive business models that offer unique value propositions.

Change is essential for ensuring the sustainability and futureproofing of businesses. Organizations can anticipate and respond to environmental, social, and regulatory changes by continuously evolving and adapting. This proactive approach helps businesses mitigate risks, seize emerging opportunities, and maintain their relevance over the long term.

In business, production always comes first. When the product is being produced with precision successfully, you commit marketing dollars behind the sales force to create new customers and convert them into new orders while stimulating and incentivizing the existing customer base to tell family, friends, and others about your product.

Formal management organizational structures emerged as a science in the 1950s and better developed techniques in the 1980s, 2000s, and 2020s. Organizational charts became a must. Taken from the military, the "chain of command" became a must for every business organization. So, there has been an evolution of putting structure into your company, allowing it to grow bigger.

I have met so many small business operators who resist structure. "This is why I started my own business because I hate structure" is what I have heard a lot of new entrepreneurs saying. Having this kind of organizational mindset is what is going to keep your company the same size for a long time!

Without structure, you cannot keep pace and grow your company by 20% or more per year. Today, you have to set the tone for your structure with the ideas of inclusivity and teamwork. We are all a family working for the same company with a common focus and purpose of delivering good things to loyal customers. We have systems in place to take the customer base upward with more structure and proven techniques supported by software that is designed to accomplish the task.

The primary purpose of an organizational chart in a business is to visually represent the structure of the organization, including its hierarchy, relationships, and lines of authority.

An organizational chart helps define and communicate the roles and responsibilities of individuals within the organization. It provides a clear picture of who reports to whom in the chain of command, reducing confusion and promoting accountability.

The chart facilitates efficient communication by identifying key decision makers and showing the flow of information within the organization. Employees can understand the reporting lines and know who to approach for specific matters.

The organizational chart helps in resource allocation, as it shows the distribution of personnel across different departments or teams. It enables managers to assess the workload, identify potential gaps, and make informed decisions about staffing and resource allocation. It shows employees' structure and communication lines and their job is to stay within their boundaries, except in extraordinary circumstances.

The chart allows management to identify skill gaps or imbalances within departments or teams by visualizing the organizational structure. This insight helps in succession planning, identifying areas where additional training or hiring may be required to ensure a smooth transition of roles and responsibilities.

The organizational chart clarifies decision making authority and facilitates the delegation of tasks. Managers can quickly identify the appropriate person to delegate specific responsibilities, ensuring efficient decision making and reducing bottlenecks.

As businesses grow, the organizational chart becomes increasingly important. It provides a roadmap for scaling operations by illustrating how new positions or departments fit into the existing structure, ensuring a seamless integration of new roles and functions.

An organizational chart is a valuable tool for promoting organizational clarity, communication, and efficiency. It helps employees understand their place within the organization, fosters collaboration and enables effective management of resources and decision making processes.

In general, the life cycle of a medium-sized privately owned company can be divided into several stages. While the specific stages and their durations may vary, here is a typical framework:

**Seed Stage:** This is the initial phase where the business idea is developed and the company is formed. Founders conduct market research, create a business plan, and secure initial funding.

**Start-up Stage:** In this stage, the company is launched, and operations begin. The focus is on building the product or service, acquiring customers, and establishing a market presence. Start-ups often face significant challenges and uncertainties during this stage.

**Growth Stage:** At this point, the company starts gaining traction and experiencing rapid growth. Sales and revenue increase and the customer base expands. Additional funding may be secured to support expansion and scale operations. The company may also explore strategic partnerships and alliances.

**Expansion Stage:** In this stage, the company continues to grow and expand its operations. It may enter new markets, expand its product or service offerings, and invest in infrastructure and resources. The company may also consider acquiring other businesses or merging with competitors.

**Maturity Stage:** At this stage, the company has achieved stability and a significant market share. Growth rates may slow down, and the focus shifts to maintaining profitability and optimizing operations. The company may also diversify its product line or explore new customer segments.

**Decline or Renewal Stage:** Depending on various factors, including market conditions and competition, a company may enter a decline phase. Sales and profits decrease, and the business faces challenges in maintaining its position. The company, in its present condition, may be losing relevance in the marketplace. However, companies can also choose to undergo a renewal phase by reinventing themselves, adopting new strategies, changing their product line to keep pace with current trends, or exploring new markets to regain growth.

It's important to note that these stages are not strictly linear, and companies can experience fluctuations and overlap between stages. Additionally, the duration of each stage can vary widely depending on the industry, market conditions, management decisions, and other factors.

Typically, entrepreneurs build a business from the ground up. They build from scratch by adopting the necessary measures of survival as they grow and build a business.

These well-known free thinkers do not fit well in the mold of big business with their more strict policies, procedures, and style of dress.

There is a pattern that entrepreneurs develop while they build businesses, only to later sell them to big businesses. Big businesses are better equipped to be in charge of daily operations. With their access to capital, they can infuse money into the idea of a growing regional business and quickly expand it into a national and then international business. These serial entrepreneurs may have a certain personality that is keen on getting things started, but they quickly find boredom in day-to-day management.

Note here an important fact in the marketplace. Big businesses do not want to speculate; they do not want to assume risk in starting something new. Big businesses hang out and look for a product that is selling well in the marketplace, then come by with a lot of cash and make offers to small companies.

Small companies are available to switch, change, pivot, and adjust overnight. Small companies can develop and perfect a process. The climbing and growing is what adds spark to the life of the entrepreneur. On the other hand, entrepreneurs are not well versed in day-to-day management. They do not have access to large sums of capital.

The trend is that small companies develop products, and then when sales are looking brisk, big companies become involved because they have access to large sums of capital, and their structure is well suited for day-to-day management. So small companies take risks, invent, develop, and perfect, and then big companies are well positioned to grow the company into an international brand.

Typically, the entrepreneur has the spirit and enthusiasm to develop the business but lacks the access to capital to grow the business internationally. This has now created a whole industry of venture capitalists.

There are groups around the country with lots of cash and access to more cash that will take an ownership position in your company and, in exchange, will put an agreed amount of cash into your business immediately with some promises to add more financing for all purchase orders, that your company can produce. Sometimes, these venture capital people will participate in the management and growth of the company and get on the phone and call key contacts to make available shelf space for your product.

To attract venture capital, you need a good idea, a business plan, and demonstrate credibility in being able to carry out the business as planned. Venture capital has a cousin in the marketplace called private equity.

They both work off of similar principles. Give up ownership, gain cash to cover start-up or sustain losses during the early growth years, then eventually make profits. Some agreements contain buy-out clauses with formulas for how to determine the value of the company at the end of a stated term, such as ten years.

As an entrepreneur, you have to be careful that the contract or the maneuvers of the venture capital people do not cause you to become ousted from the company. Many entrepreneurs with good ideas bled losses for five years; they were carried on the backs of venture capital groups. In year seven, after two years of profitability, they tossed out the entrepreneur and installed a "real CEO" to run the company.

For those new college entrepreneurs who graduated with a written business plan, be careful when making contracts with venture capital groups in the first, second, and third rounds of financing. Study the ups and downs of Uber and 50 other similar companies with ousted founders of the company.

Big business is afraid of pouring money into a new idea to develop a product that has no proof of concept, no known customers, and no one knows if the product is going to work or not. Will there be customer acceptance of this new product? Big business turns away from start-ups but embraces a business activity they can do over and over again with their team of professional day-to-day managers.

Entrepreneurship attracts a person with the spirit and energy to undertake a hands on start and develop a business from scratch. Developing the product building sales and survival tactics grows the company into a viable business that, through its own inertia, is organically growing and prospering in the marketplace

Innovation is the process of discovering new products and ideas that can be used in business. Sometimes, an entrepreneur is not an innovator; most of the time, the innovator is not an entrepreneur.

**CHAPTER 11**

# How To Purchase a Business

Key things to know when buying a business…

Buying a business from a business broker can be a significant undertaking for a new entrepreneur. It's essential to approach the process with caution and diligence to ensure you make a sound investment. Here are some key things to be careful and cautious of as you work through your due diligence checklist.

Don't solely rely on the information provided by the business broker. Conduct your due diligence to verify all the claims made about the business, including its financials, assets, liabilities, and market position. Be sure the business is not failing due to its rent factor or location. Get a copy of the existing lease, go talk with the landlord to get a long-term lease with 5-year options to renew. Be convincing that your business cannot withstand annual increases in the rent.

Some businesses may have underlying issues or pending legal liabilities that are not immediately apparent. Hire a professional accountant and attorney to help you identify any potential problems before closing the deal. When you close, you will have a legally prepared buy-sell agreement. This agreement should seal you off from any liabilities, debts, and unpaid taxes from the old owner, the seller.

Business brokers may overvalue a business to attract potential buyers. Conduct an independent valuation of the business to ensure you are paying a fair price based on its true worth. Some businesses sell based upon a multiple of the sales, and some businesses sell based upon a multiple of the net profit, excluding the salary and all the benefits of the seller.

You should be able to calculate the valuation method used and come to your own conclusion that the price you offer is a fair amount. Become familiar with the difference between an asset sale and a regular sale. The regular sale will include the information to be able to make and market the product and a one-year agreement that the seller will be available to answer all questions about making and shipping the product in the future. There are also franchise purchase opportunities that will allow you to get coaching and information on how to run the business from the seller for one year and from the franchisor year after year, forever.

Understand the seller's real reason for selling the business. It could be due to declining performance, increased competition, or other significant issues. Make sure you know the true motivation behind the sale.

Ensure the seller signs a non-compete agreement, preventing them from starting a similar business nearby and taking away customers or employees. Non-compete agreements are very tricky and governed under state law. You will need your own lawyer to read and explain the intricacies of the non-compete agreement that you offer to the seller. Design the non-compete so that it will stick and prohibit the seller or seller's family from direct competition with your new company.

Analyze the financial records of the business carefully to ensure it is in good standing with tax authorities and has been compliant with all financial obligations. Be wary if the seller says they don't keep or don't have the past records. You are entitled to see the business bank statements, canceled checks (or equivalents), and all the paid and unpaid invoices for the business for the last five years. The seller may also offer to show you the income and sales tax returns filed with the related taxing authorities.

Review existing contracts with customers and employees to understand any obligations or potential risks that come with the business. This should also be covered in your buy-sell agreement. The seller may offer a complete list and digital database of the customers of the business one day before the close of escrow once all of the other contingencies have been removed.

Part of your due diligence checklist should include your assessment of the potential for future growth and sustainability of the business. Evaluate the market conditions and industry trends that may impact the business positively or negatively. Get a traffic and demographic study of the area to be sure your target customer is within easy reach of the business location. Evaluate customer parking opportunities and your shipping and delivery requirements.

Be cautious about the terms of any financing deals offered by the broker. Compare them with other financing options available to you to ensure you get the best deal possible. Sometimes, with collateral, the seller will provide some financing for the business.

Don't be afraid to negotiate the terms and conditions of the deal to protect your interests and minimize risks. You will want to cut the best deal possible. Therefore, you should be sharp and offer reasons why you offer less than the asking price.

Remember that the broker's primary goal is to facilitate the transaction and earn a commission. While they can provide valuable assistance, they usually represent the seller's interests. Consider hiring your broker to represent your side of the deal, called a buyer's broker. This may be a wise choice, as one broker may know how to call foul on the other! The alternative is to have a buyer's broker in the background and you do all the negotiation with the tips and information your broker/consultant offers to you.

Avoid making hasty decisions based on emotions. Take your time to think critically and assess the business objectively. This is a business purchase and not an emotional purchase. You will need a pad of paper and a spreadsheet to come to the right conclusions as to the valuation used to purchase the business. Don't sit back and learn about all of this five years after you paid too much for the business to begin with.

Buying a business can be a rewarding venture, but it's crucial to be diligent, ask the right questions, and seek professional advice when needed. Remember, the success of your entrepreneurial journey depends significantly on the choices you make at the outset.

Find a business broker you like to deal with, explain that you want to start a business, and examine their listings on their website. Most everyone, including a seller of a business, runs from someone new to self-employment. Don't be disenchanted. Believe in yourself. Know that you can do it. Once involved, whether it's shoes, snow cones, tacos, electronic devices, or hamburgers, once in the business, you can learn about the product, the industry, and what is drawing business to your location; then, with this knowledge, serve the customers well.

The next step is working with the existing employees and then learning how to recruit talent. You don't want people to fill a space; you want people who will become a team player on your team. You have to be the coach and develop a team of people who will learn the key focus of the business and carry out the plan all day when you are busy with something else. Set in place appropriate systems and procedures.

It is up to you to further develop the business. Have the business sell the existing products while determining which new things to add to your product line. Your next steps are to get to know the customers and ask them why they are there, what they like, what they don't like. As the new owner, they usually will tell you everything, so be sure to listen to improve. Then, make customer satisfaction and customer loyalty a priority.

Outside contacts from outside of your business can help your business grow. A key call to Costco, Walmart, Target, and many more might help you sell more products. It's fun to watch the show "Shark Tank." There are entrepreneurs who come to the show without much camera training.

They tell the sharks about their product and its function in the marketplace. Then, they explain who needs the product and why. Then a shark bites. Then, on Monday morning, the shark is on the phone with Costco, Walmart, Target, and many more stores, getting more orders for the product while the shark stands ready to finance (put money up) for new purchase orders.

The money in advance from the shark enables the business to purchase the raw material, assemble the material using its labor force and equipment, and then deliver a quality product to the store that placed the order. Notice the flow. In this example, it's get the order, make the product, deliver the product, collect the purchase price, and then get poised and ready for the next order. With the customer payment, you receive money to pay for the cost of the product, pay for your overhead, and pay your salary. Put the money back into the business in order to make these payments while making the next batch of products. You have to know the flow and the principles of cash flow for the business.

The sharks know that they cannot create orders for more products than the labor force, and the equipment can make in an agreed upon period. By accepting orders, making the product, collecting for the product, then step by step, they can grow the company into a newer, bigger, more modern facility, now able to accept more and larger orders.

Retail is a difficult space because the retailer wants your product to "sell through" the store. The retail store wants your product to fly off the shelf and create empty space for you to fill with new products. Retail computers keep track of what is selling and what is not. They can cancel your space if your product is not selling through.

Through your efforts of buying a business, assembling a team, making a product or service, selling the product or service. Then, using marketing skills, awaken the public's awareness of the availability of the product. Then you have mastered the full cycle of taking raw material, turning it into a salable product, and making your target market aware the product is available. You have learned the full cycle of the marketing and production side of owning a business.

When some people buy a business, they fall down because they have some idea that they just sit back and let the employees make the product. There are a lot more steps to running a business. You have to use your time to LEARN more about the industry and how to make your target customer aware of the availability of the product.

In management consulting work, I am often invited into a business to explain why the business is not growing. Our report sometimes explains that they do not have an active, alive, enthusiastic marketing department. The reaction of the business owner is: "We cannot afford to do this."

Wait a minute, the business you have owned for five years is stagnant and has had the same amount of sales for the last three years. You want the business to grow, but you do not want to think about marketing steps? The vital steps of letting people who are not using your product or service know about what you do and how you can help them. If you tell more people and 10% of those come to buy your product or service, they each have five friends who can use your product. Through the mathematical rules of "multiple progression," in one year's time, you will have a lot more customers than you have today.

The businesses that fail are those that have stagnated or declining sales. They are afraid to reach out to consultants to help their business grow. They try to continue in business while watching their existing sales sink.

Each year, producing less sales than the year before, soon reaches a point where they have to use their savings and retirement funds to keep the business afloat. After a few years of business losses, they give up and close the doors, or for the more stubborn ones, the landlord does not receive the rent; therefore, the landlord has to toss them out, and then the doors close and back to the 8 to 5 job they go.

Here are some of the key reasons that small start-up businesses fail. Small start-up entrepreneurs can fail due to a multitude of reasons, often stemming from their inherent challenges and business environment. They become overwhelmed and fail to learn about, standard business systems and procedures, the product quality and the customers' needs.

Inadequate market research can lead to a mismatch between the product and actual customer needs. Insufficient funding and financial mismanagement can cripple operations and growth potential. A lack of a viable business model and clear value proposition can hinder customer acquisition and revenue generation.

Poor management, including a lack of experience and leadership, can undermine decision making and overall direction. Intense competition and failure to differentiate and compete in a business like way can impede market entry and growth.

Additionally, startups can fail due to ineffective marketing strategies, leading to low visibility and customer engagement. A failure to adapt to changing market dynamics and pivot, when necessary, can also be detrimental. Owner's conflicts and team issues, such as co-founder (spousal) disputes and talent gaps, can disrupt operations and company culture. Moreover, regulatory challenges and legal issues can arise, causing unexpected setbacks. Rapid scaling without a solid infrastructure can strain resources and lead to operational breakdowns.

Some analysts say failure is due to bad management and lack of capital. The failure to do something positive each day to know and keep customers satisfied. The failure to identify to change or find new products or offerings for the customer base.

Successful startups address these challenges through comprehensive research, learning, strategic planning, efficient resource allocation, continuous innovation, and adaptable strategies. They also cultivate a skilled and motivated team while staying attuned to market feedback and evolving trends.

These failures are written about in financial magazines and newspapers as another statistic of a new business that meets with failure. If you hustle and find out what can change or be adjusted or improved, you will have a vital business with growing sales. If all you want to do is stand in your store and go home, you have not performed the business development steps as an entrepreneur.

The steps to success are to take a product or service, present it to the marketplace, and serve well the existing customers, but have a vital function of gathering new customers to purchase the product.

It's really that simple. These are not complicated steps, though they are vital steps. You have to be actively involved with your business. If you have idle time, you are not managing, evolving, and learning in your business very well.

CHAPTER 12

# Financing, Venture Capital and Private Equity

The importance of capital markets for small and medium-sized private companies and how to access capital is very important for a business owner to know how to traverse this landscape. Here's a simplified explanation of where to look for capital with a private company.

**Capital Markets:** Capital markets are where buyers and sellers trade financial instruments such as stocks, bonds, and other securities. These markets serve as a mechanism for raising capital (money) for businesses and provide investors with opportunities to grow their wealth. In the context of small and medium-sized private companies, capital markets offer various avenues to secure funding.

**Survival and Expansion:** Small and medium-sized businesses often face unique challenges. They may lack the resources and financial stability of larger corporations, making them more vulnerable to economic downturns, competitive pressures, and unforeseen crises. Access to capital becomes crucial for several reasons:

**Working Capital:** Adequate working capital is essential for daily operations, paying suppliers, employees, and covering overhead costs. Without it, businesses may struggle to meet their short-term obligations.

**Investment in Growth:** To expand, small and medium-sized companies need funds for research and development, marketing, technology upgrades, and geographic expansion. Capital markets provide a means to raise these funds.

**Innovation and Competitiveness:** Access to capital enables businesses to invest in innovation, stay competitive, and adapt to changing market conditions. This agility is essential for long-term survival.

**Risk Management:** Diversifying sources of capital can help mitigate risks. Over-reliance on a single source, such as a bank loan or a single investor, can expose a business to financial instability if that source dries up.

Types of Capital Markets for Small and Medium-sized Companies: These are the options available to privately held companies. With some creativity there are other options but let's discuss various capital market options tailored to the needs of small and medium-sized enterprises (SMEs):

**Private Equity:** SMEs can attract investments from private equity firms or venture capitalists. These investors provide capital in exchange for equity ownership or a share of the company's profits. Private equity can help businesses grow and innovate.

**Debt Financing:** Companies can raise capital by issuing bonds or securing loans from banks or non-bank lenders. Debt financing allows businesses to access funds without giving up ownership but requires regular interest payments.

**IPOs and Public Markets:** Some SMEs choose to go public through an initial public offering (IPO). This involves listing shares on stock exchanges, allowing them to raise capital from a broader base of investors. Public markets provide liquidity and visibility.

**Alternative Financing:** Crowdfunding, peer-to-peer lending, and other innovative financing methods are becoming popular options for SMEs, offering access to capital without the need for traditional intermediaries.

**SBA:** The Small Business Administration, an independent agency of the federal government to aid, counsel, assist and protect the interests of small business. By application and acceptance, the SBA guarantees business loans that are funded by local, regional and national banks.

**Challenges and Considerations:** It's important to note that accessing capital markets isn't without challenges. SMEs may face regulatory hurdles, disclosure requirements, and the need to demonstrate a strong business case to attract investors. Additionally, presentation, analytical and financial management skills become critical to navigate these markets effectively.

Access to capital through capital markets is a vital lifeline for small and medium-sized private companies. It provides the resources needed for survival, growth, and competitiveness in the dynamic business landscape. However, businesses must carefully evaluate their financing options and strategies to make the most of these opportunities. Qualification for a loan through having a relevant product or service and a good business track record is a speedy way to get financed.

Let's discuss and focus on what help private equity firms and venture capital firms can play in providing capital to privately held companies.

In various stages of business, venture capital and, lately, private equity firms will give money to a business in exchange for a list of promises. They give money because they believe in; the company, the product, the management team, and the team's ability to work hard and execute well.

With their experienced vision, they see an opportunity for this company to grow rapidly in the marketplace. Some of the promises the current business owners give are for:

an undiluted amount of the company stock, promises are about meeting certain growth targets promises may be about a specified buy-out date and the terms of the buy-out promises of going public with the stock can be part of the deal.

- Robust ROI: Commitment to delivering substantial returns on investment.

- Transparent Communication: Regular updates and open dialogue on company progress.

- Efficient Resource Allocation: Prudent use of funds to maximize growth.

- Scalability Focus: Strategies aimed at rapid expansion.

- Risk Mitigation: Proactive measures to manage potential risks.

- Ethical Practices: Upholding strong ethical standards in all operations.

- Investor Collaboration: Collaboration in key decisions for mutual success.

## Financing, Venture Capital And Private Equity / 213

A venture capital (VC) firm or private equity (PE) firm provides businesses with investment capital to facilitate expansion and navigate the crucial growth period for several compelling reasons.

In business and in growing a business access to capital is vitally important. One of the most important things to know when managing a business.

Access to capital is a cornerstone of any business enterprise. It not only facilitates the inception and initial growth phase, but also underpins expansion, innovation, and risk mitigation. All business in all stages of their life cycle need access to capital.

Without capital, businesses face stifled growth, constrained potential, and heightened vulnerability. In the dynamic landscape of global business, where competition is fierce and markets are continually evolving, capital acts as a lifeline.

It enables businesses to leverage opportunities, adapt to challenges, and cultivate resilience. Beyond mere survival, strategic capital allocation can significantly enhance competitive advantage, fueling differentiation and long-term sustainability. In essence, access to capital is not just important, it's imperative for business success.

VC and PE firms seek businesses with high growth potential. They invest in companies that have demonstrated promising market traction, unique, innovative ideas, and scalable business models. By injecting capital, these businesses can scale their operations, enter new markets, and maximize their growth potential.

VC and PE firms invest in businesses with the expectation of generating substantial returns. They carefully select companies that show promising growth prospects, aiming for a significant increase in valuation over a relatively short period. By providing the necessary capital, these firms help businesses achieve rapid growth, thereby enhancing the likelihood of attractive returns on their investments.

When you stop and analyze most all Fortune 500 companies sought venture capital at one time or another. Once large enough a company can also go the public market with corporate securities such as bonds.

Public companies can raise funds from the public marketplace through various types of loans and securities offerings. Common options include:

- Corporate Bonds: Issuing bonds to investors, which are debt securities with fixed interest rates and maturity dates.

- Commercial Paper: Short-term unsecured promissory notes often used for working capital needs.

- Convertible Debt: Bonds that can be converted into company stock at a predetermined price.

- Preferred Stock: Offering shares with preferential dividend rights.

- Securitized Loans: Bundling loans into securities for sale.

- Rights Offerings: Allowing existing shareholders to buy additional shares.

- Initial Public Offerings (IPOs): Selling shares to the public for the first time.

These options provide public companies with diverse financing avenues to support their operations and growth.

Non-public companies vitally need access to capital to grow but when they look around, they are somewhat limited to family, friends, rich uncles, larger companies in their industry, industry suppliers then venture capital.

Non-public companies, often referred to as private companies, have several options for raising expansion capital. The choice of method will depend on the company's specific needs, its growth stage, industry, and risk tolerance. Here are some common avenues for private companies to secure expansion capital:

1. **Bootstrapping:** Self-funding the growth of the company using existing profits or personal savings. This approach allows the founders to maintain control and ownership.

2. **Angel Investors:** Angel investors are high-net-worth individuals who provide capital in exchange for equity ownership in the company. They often offer expertise and connections in addition to funding.

3. **Venture Capital:** If the company has substantial growth potential, it can seek venture capital funding. Venture capitalists (VCs) provide funding in exchange for equity and are often interested in high-growth tech startups and innovative businesses.

4. **Private Equity:** Private equity firms invest in mature private companies, often with the goal of taking them to the next level. They may buy a significant stake in the company and work closely with management to grow it leaving the founders with royalty and licensing agreements.

5. **Family and Friends:** Some entrepreneurs turn to family members and close friends to raise initial capital. This should be done carefully to avoid straining personal relationships.

6. **Crowdfunding:** Equity crowdfunding platforms allow private companies to raise capital from a large number of individual investors in exchange for equity or debt. This approach can be suitable for early-stage businesses.

7. **Bank Loans and Lines of Credit:** Private companies with a strong financial track record may qualify for traditional bank loans or lines of credit. These typically require collateral and come with interest payments.

8. **Alternative Lenders:** There are alternative lending options, such as online lenders and peer-to-peer lending platforms, that provide access to capital with different terms than traditional banks. Beware of fees and interest rates and any changes to the interest rate in the loan contract.

9. **Strategic Partnerships:** Forming strategic partnerships with other companies can provide not only capital but also access to new markets, customers, or technology.

10. **Grants and Competitions:** Some industries and regions offer grants, subsidies, or awards for specific types of businesses, innovations, or research projects. Look for state and federal government programs, industry associations, or competitions.

11. **Convertible Notes and SAFE (Simple Agreement for Future Equity):** These financial instruments allow companies to raise capital without immediately determining the valuation. They convert into equity at a later funding round or event.

12. **Revenue Based Financing:** Some companies offer revenue-based financing, where they provide capital in exchange for a percentage of future revenues until a predetermined cap is reached.

13. **Mezzanine Financing:** Mezzanine financing is a hybrid of debt and equity, typically used by established companies. It involves loans with the option to convert into equity if certain conditions are met.

14. **Private Placements:** Private placements involve selling securities to a select group of accredited investors. This method is often used for larger capital raises.

15. **Secondary Markets:** Some private companies use secondary markets for selling shares to accredited investors, providing liquidity to early investors and employees.

The choice of funding source will depend on factors such as the company's stage of growth, business model, valuation, and the level of control the founders are willing to relinquish. It's essential to carefully evaluate each option, seek legal, securities and financial advice, and develop a comprehensive business plan when seeking expansion capital for a private company.

VC and PE firms bring valuable expertise, industry knowledge, and networks to the businesses they invest in. They often have extensive experience in specific business sectors and can provide strategic guidance, mentorship, and operational support to help businesses overcome growth challenges. Their network of contacts can open doors to potential partnerships, customers, and further investment opportunities.

Expanding and navigating through the growth phase can be challenging for a business. VC and PE firms can help mitigate some of the investment risks by diversifying their investment portfolios across multiple companies. They often invest in a range of businesses, spreading their risk and increasing the likelihood of overall portfolio success.

During the growth period, businesses require capital to invest in key areas such as research and development, marketing, talent acquisition, production, and infrastructure. VC and PE firms provide the necessary funding to accelerate these initiatives and help businesses capitalize on emerging opportunities. The capital infusion can also support working capital needs, debt repayment, and other financial obligations, ensuring the business has the necessary resources to thrive.

VC and PE firms invest in businesses during the growth phase to capitalize on their potential, generate attractive returns, provide expertise and networks, mitigate risk, and facilitate the necessary capital infusion for expansion. This partnership between the investor and the business aligns their interests and paves the way for mutual success.

If we had enough paper and ink, one could write wild tales of the dramatic ups and downs of companies involved with venture capitalists. Business growth does not always go smoothly when you are trying to build a nationwide or international firm.

Venture capital starts with a well-spoken person giving a pitch to a group of venture capitalists. The talk is supported by a thick, well documented business plan, samples of the product or service, and a well-defined outline of what the business is going to accomplish.

Can you imagine Jeff Bezos in 1999 coming into a room and saying that he was in the book business and wanted to expand his business into a worldwide warehouse full of many household and electronic things? I am sure laughter would have filled the room. The initial start-up capital for Amazon.com came primarily from his parents, who invested a large amount of their life savings in what became Amazon.com.

Jeff founded his company in stages, with the help of rounds of funding, over criticism of where the profit for this business was when he came back asking for more. Building a business is like "building blocks," one block at a time, then you end up with the finished product. Much like building step by step.

There are different levels of funding rounds:

- pre-seed funding,
- seed funding,
- series A funding,
- series B funding,
- series C funding,

Sometimes startups proceed with series D and E rounds of funding. The seed funding round and series A, B, and C are the four official funding stages.

Asking too much from the venture capital people is a bad idea. They have to see things in squares, like in a box, in which they are comfortable and familiar with. They see, here is a Harvard and Wharton team of two who put together this whiz-bang business plan and want to go out into the world and turn hydrogen into water.

When making the pitch to raise capital for a start-up business, early-stage investors can be very hard to find. When you are granted a meeting, it might be difficult to get funded.

When they hear a pitch, the venture capitalists are looking for people with a concept, and they often see people who have no proof this idea will work. The way certain things are pitched may ring home as a good idea to take a chance on.

New companies may have no sales. The founders just graduated from school with no ten-year proven track record as a CEO while holding up a popsicle stick example of what the final product might look like. However, it is possible to get funded if something clicks with one or more of the investors.

There are people with no sales, a drawing of the product, no proof of concept, wanting $10 million for 2% of their company. Venture capital groups are known for making large bets on a new company in the hope of hitting a home run with the prospect that the business may turn into a billion-dollar company one day.

The venture capital group looks at the business plan, the grades of the founders, and information as to what they did in high school to excel at everything they did. The group eventually will look at the business plan, the proposed management team, and what exactly is going to be made over what timeframe.

The venture capital people will likely do their own market research and make various phone calls to experts who know about the product or service. VC people do their homework and conduct independent research through their own channels to then come back and test the accuracy of the contents of the business plan.

All of this collected data is then considered in a private meeting of only the VC people. The parties know that they are taking a risk, but somehow, the VCs have the risk covered if things go in the wrong direction. The pitch may be for a product or industry the group is familiar with, and the group already has a large host of experts who can be on the phone to put out fires if there is a need.

The VCs are looking for a solid founder who is credible and can be trusted to carry out and execute the business plan on time and on schedule.

The entrepreneur founder is looking for money from heaven to fund their idea. This type of lending is well beyond the ability of a bank to assume this amount of risk. The VCs are in the business of accepting risk. Usually, the VC firm has experts and contacts who can provide assistance as needed with or without the knowledge of the founder operator. When funded, the founder is given a green light, a pile of money, and is granted the right to proceed, following; a path and the very clear terms of the deal that has been struck.

Uber was another tumultuous venture capital funded business. The founding CEO was originally looked at as someone who could bulldoze through the regulatory bodies that wanted to tax and license UBER as they did tax, regulate, and license taxi cabs.

UBER had battles to fight from the beginning and still has battles to contend with today, partially because the categorization of the UBER driver as an independent contractor versus an employee has become a large issue.

In the middle of all of this, the founder CEO of Uber got tossed out of his CEO position based on the demands of the investors, which were based on concerns about the behavior of the CEO.

Mr. Kalanick was forced to resign as chief executive in 2017 after a series of privacy scandals and complaints of discrimination and sexual harassment at the company.

This amount of turmoil caused the investors grave concern. One day, UBER was a great idea; another day, England attacked UBER, and then a British court ruled. The court ruled that drivers were to be classified as workers and are entitled to rights such as holiday pay. The legal battle began in 2016 when two ex-Uber drivers argued they should receive holiday pay and minimum wage.

In India and other countries, too, many drivers were giving rides to women who reported getting mistreated instead of a ride directly to their destination.

There is a long list of companies that ultimately became successful companies that had to jump through rings of fire to stay in business, continue to grow sales, and ultimately achieve a profit in order to continue to keep the doors open.

Venture capital and private equity are powerful. They are capable of making deals with restaurants or manufacturing companies. Well known to us is a restaurant that a private equity firm bought out. The private equity firm quickly formed a management team and took a local restaurant made up of three locations. Within one year, the restaurant, branded under a new name but using the recipes of the acquired company, had 125 locations. All locations looked the same, and food uniformity was within tolerance. So, a small business becomes a big business within 12 months, showing a bystander the power and strength of equity investors.

Largely, investment firms are funding companies through the heavy growth stage of the company's life cycle, and many are from the initial startup through this heavy growth stage.

Managing a company through a heavy growth stage can be challenging for experienced CEOs due to several factors:

Rapid growth often brings increased complexity to various aspects of the business, such as operations, supply chain, customer acquisition, and internal processes. The CEO must navigate through these complexities and ensure that the company's systems, procedures, infrastructure, and organizational structure can support and scale with the growth. This requires making strategic decisions, implementing efficient processes, and maintaining effective communication across the organization.

As a company grows, the CEO needs to attract and retain top talent to fill key roles. This can be challenging in a competitive market where skilled individuals are in high demand. Finding the right people who align with the company's values and culture, possess the necessary skills, and can handle the increased demands of a rapidly growing organization becomes crucial.

Managing talent acquisition, onboarding, and retention strategies becomes a significant responsibility for the CEO and the employees who are delegated this task. Joining a highly leveraged growth company can be risky from the employee perspective. Other employees see hope and promise and demand stock options to give them more wealth if the company succeeds the other side. These employees believe in themselves to contribute in a positive way to the company's chances of making it through the growth stage.

Rapid growth often requires substantial investments in resources, infrastructure, technology, and talent. With the CFO's delegated help, the CEO must effectively manage the company's finances to ensure adequate capital is available to support growth initiatives. This involves forecasting cash flow, managing budgets, securing additional funding if necessary, and maintaining financial discipline to avoid potential pitfalls associated with overextension or inadequate resources.

Growth brings new opportunities and challenges, and CEOs must make critical decisions that shape the company's future. However, the speed and uncertainty of growth can make decision making more difficult. CEOs may need to rely on incomplete information, take calculated risks, make assumptions and adapt quickly to changing market dynamics. The consequences of these decisions can significantly impact the company's trajectory, making the decision making process more complex and demanding.

As a company grows, preserving the original culture and values that contributed to its initial success becomes increasingly challenging. The CEO must actively work to ensure the company's culture remains intact, even as new employees join and the organizational structure evolves. Maintaining a cohesive and aligned culture and values becomes crucial for employee engagement, productivity, and long-term success.

The processes and systems that worked well during the early stages of a company may not be suitable for managing rapid growth. CEOs must evaluate and restructure various aspects of the organization, including operations, technology, and internal communication, to support scalability. This requires implementing efficient systems, optimizing workflows, and developing robust infrastructure to support the increased demands of a growing company.

Overall, managing a company through a heavy growth stage demands strong leadership, strategic thinking, adaptability, and the ability to balance short-term priorities with long-term goals. Experienced CEOs face these challenges as they navigate the complexities of growth, ensuring that the company maintains its trajectory and capitalizes on opportunities while managing risks effectively.

Throughout this chapter we will switch back and forth between a VC and a PE firm and what they do and how they do it and what differentiates them. I am sure the question about what the differences are will be on the test at the end.

A private equity firm refers to an investment company that utilizes its own funds or capital from other investors for its expansion and startup operations. Private Equity firms are usually not listed publicly, and their shares are not traded in the stock market.

For this reason, private equity firms are not subject to a majority of the regulations that public companies need to comply with. Often referred to as a financial sponsor, the firm will raise capital to invest according to specific investment strategies.

Normally, the firm has a specific theme. Then, the firm attracts money for future investment from pension plans and other avenues with a large amount of money to invest, and it wants to earn a reasonable rate of return for its members.

The pension plan hopes to make a 10%+ return on its invested capital. The Private Equity firm hopes to make business expansion investments and tries to earn a 60%+ return on its investment. You can see what happens: the pension plan puts up the money, and the private equity firm invests the money. The private equity firm makes a 60% return on the investment and, in turn, pays the pension plan 12%. The extra 48% is profit for the private equity firm to keep paying its business expenses and pay salaries to its employees.

The home run for the private equity firm is to invest in a struggling company. Get control of the management of the company. Examine the expenses of the company and eliminate the expenses that do not lead directly to making more sales or expenses that are not making production happen more efficiently. This means the three jets go away, and the expensive cars, club membership, and skyboxes all go away.

Once the private equity firm and its hired managers clean up the company, they go to work to improve sales. Once sales show an improvement, they offer the shares of the company for sale in an initial public offering (IPO). At the end of the day, the private equity firm can potentially make a 700% return on its invested capital. The firm pays its investor, the pension plan, a 12% return on its invested capital. It can keep the remaining 688% for future investment, business expenses, and employee salaries and bonuses.

Exiting from the companies, which private equity firm invests in, at a sizeable profit, is usually the end goal of private equity firms. The exit often happens three to seven years after the initial investment, though it may take more or less time, depending on the strategic situation. Value is captured at exit through cutting costs, paying down debt used in funding the transaction, growing revenue during the holding period, optimizing working capital, and selling the company at a higher price than when it was acquired.

Most exits result from an acquisition by a company or an IPO, with IPO acquisitions being the most popular method.

A private equity firm refers to an investment management company that offers financial backing to private companies. The equity firm invests in operating companies or a startup through a number of associated investment strategies such as venture capital, growth capital, and leveraged buyout. The goal and motivation for such commitments is the pursuit of attaining a positive return on investment. The overall goal is to exit, and the PE is not invested in a long-term buy-and-hold situation.

A private equity firm is a type of investment entity that pools capital from various investors, such as high-net-worth individuals, institutional investors, and pension funds, to acquire, invest in, or provide funding for private companies. These firms aim to enhance the performance and value of their portfolio companies over a specified holding period, typically 3-7 years, before selling them for a profit. Private equity investors commit their dollars to these firms through investment funds. These funds are managed by the private equity firm's professionals who make investment decisions, oversee portfolio companies, and ultimately distribute returns, often through capital gains and dividends, back to the investors.

Private equity firms will be given management fees periodically and receive a share in the profits earned from the managed private equity funds. Since direct investment into a company is the main goal of a private equity investment, they need a large capital outlay to acquire a substantial level of control over the operations of the firm. This is why the industry is dominated by large funds with lots of money.

Private equity funds engage in a number of functions to ensure that they get a return on their investment. They need to raise capital from limited partners or from their own money to contribute to the fund. The equity firm will then perform due diligence when analyzing potential companies for acquisition. They will also be involved in the management of the company by providing support and advice on strategy, financial management, and operations to improve the performance of the company. This will ensure that the eventual exit is profitable.

Private equity is capital invested in a company or other entity that is not publicly listed or traded.

Venture capital is funding given to startups or other young businesses that show potential for long-term growth.

Private equity is sometimes confused with venture capital because both refer to firms that invest in companies and exit by selling their investments in equity financing, for example, by holding initial stock offerings (IPOs). However, there are significant differences in the way firms involved in the two types of funding conduct business.

Private Equity (PE) and Venture Capital (VC) firms invest in different types and sizes of companies, commit different amounts of money, and claim different percentages of equity in the companies in which they invest.

Private equity is equity invested in an entity that is not publicly traded. Private equity is a source of investment capital from high-net-worth individuals and pension plans. These investors invest capital, acquire shares of private companies, or gain control of public companies with the intention of taking them private and ultimately delisting them from public stock exchanges.

This will allow them to be a private company and pour in capital, making the earnings negative. The private company is not concerned about this temporary condition. On the other hand, if the company remained a public company, then the public company's stock price would decline sharply due to a lack of positive earnings during this revamping stage.

Large institutional investors dominate the private equity world, including pension funds and large private equity firms funded by a group of accredited investors. Many times, these people know each other or have worked with each other before. One of the key duties of the private equity firm is to establish relationships with people, institutions or funds that have a lot of cash to invest. Sometimes, these are individuals, and sometimes, the private equity customer is an institution of some kind.

Venture capital is financing given to start-up companies and small businesses that are seen as having the potential to generate high rates of growth and above-average returns, often fueled by innovation or by creating a new industry niche.

Venture capital is available for early-stage financing, business expansion financing, and acquisition/buyout financing.

A venture capital (VC) firm and a private equity (PE) firm are both types of investment firms, but they differ in their focus, investment strategies, and stages of investment.

A venture capital firm primarily invests in early-stage and high-growth companies. It aims to identify innovative startups with significant growth potential and provides them with the necessary capital and resources to scale their operations. VC firms often invest in industries such as technology, biotech, and disruptive sectors. They typically take equity stakes in the companies they invest in and actively participate in their management and strategic decision making. Most of the time, the VC's ownership is less than 50% of the ownership of the company it invests in.

On the other hand, a private equity firm focuses on investing in more mature companies that have already established a track record and are seeking capital for expansion, restructuring, or acquisitions. PE firms invest in a wide range of industries and often acquire a controlling stake in the companies they invest in. They aim to improve operational efficiency, enhance profitability, and generate returns through strategies such as buyouts, recapitalizations, and turnarounds.

Venture capital firms specialize in early-stage, high-growth startups. In contrast, private equity firms target more established companies with the aim of driving operational improvements and generating returns through various investment strategies.

Private equity firms and venture capital (VC) firms typically raise capital from different sources, although there can be some overlap.

## Private Equity Firms:

**Institutional Investors:** Private equity firms primarily raise capital from institutional investors such as pension funds, endowments, insurance companies, and sovereign wealth funds. These institutions allocate a portion of their assets to private equity investments, seeking higher returns over the long term.

**High-Net-Worth Individuals:** Private equity firms may also attract capital from high-net-worth individuals (HNWIs) who have significant investable assets. Some private equity firms have dedicated funds or vehicles specifically targeted at HNWIs.

**Fund Structure:** Private equity firms typically raise capital through closed-end funds with a fixed duration. Limited partners (investors) commit capital to the fund, and the private equity firm draws from that committed capital as needed for investments.

## Venture Capital Firms:

1. **Limited Partners:** Venture capital firms raise capital from limited partners, similar to private equity firms. However, the composition of limited partners can be slightly different. While institutional investors are still a significant source, VC firms may also

attract funding from angel investors, family offices, and corporate investors.

2. **Emphasis on Technology Startups:** VC firms focus on early-stage or high-growth companies, particularly in the technology sector. They seek out innovative startups with the potential for substantial growth and typically provide both funding and strategic guidance. However, some firms specialize in other industries.

3. **Fund Structure:** Venture capital funds can also be structured as closed-end funds, but they often have a more flexible investment approach. VC firms may have multiple funds with different focuses or stages of investment (e.g., seed, Series A, etc.). Some venture capital firms also operate as "evergreen" funds, continuously raising and deploying capital without a fixed lifespan.

Private equity firms predominantly raise capital from institutional investors and HNWIs through closed-end funds, while venture capital firms attract capital from a mix of institutional investors, angel investors, family offices, and corporate investors, often with a focus on technology startups.

For venture capital firms, the funding for this type of financing usually comes from wealthy investors, investment banks, and specialized VC funds. The investment does not have to be financial but can also be offered via technical or managerial expertise. Many times, someone sells a lot of their shares of Apple or Google, now they have a lot of cash, and then they start their own venture capital firm. Notice these key shareholders would have a lot of industry expertise to use to figure out if the VC applicant has a slight chance of making it in the marketplace. Then, if their VC money is invested, the key employee VC investor is there with their expertise and network of friends to help the new company become successful.

For newer companies or those with a short operating history, let's say four years or less, venture capital funding is both popular and sometimes necessary for raising capital. This is particularly the case if the new company does not have access to capital markets, bank loans, or other debt instruments. A downside for the fledgling company is that the investors often obtain equity, a substantial percentage of the company shares of stock, in the new company, and, therefore, by agreement, they get a voice in company decisions.

A lot of the VC's ownership and control is handled by a contract entered into between the VC and the new company. Often, the new company is held over the barrel and has little choice but to cave into the demands of the venture capital firm.

Let's continue to study some of the differences between private equity and venture capital firms. Private equity firms mostly buy mature companies that are already established. The companies may be deteriorating or failing to make the profits they should due to inefficiency. Private equity firms buy these companies and streamline operations to increase revenues and earnings. Venture capital firms, on the other hand, mostly invest in startups with high growth potential.

Private equity firms mostly buy 100% ownership of the companies in which they invest. As a result, the firm is in total control of the companies after the buyout. Venture capital firms invest and then receive a given percentage, usually less than 50% of the stock of the company. Most venture capital firms prefer to spread out their risk and invest in many different companies. If one startup fails, the entire fund in the venture capital firm is not affected substantially.

Private equity firms usually invest $50 million and up in a single company. These firms prefer to concentrate all their efforts on a single company since they invest in already established and mature companies. The chances of absolute losses from such an investment are minimal. Venture capitalists typically spend $10 million or less on each company since they mostly deal with startups with unpredictable, unforecastable chances of failure or success.

Private equity firms can buy companies from any industry, while venture capital firms tend to focus their attention on start-ups in technology and biotechnology but are not in any way limited to these industries.

Where do you find a venture capital firm? There are directories that are divided by industry that will tell you what the VC firms are looking for. There are apps that may direct you to a venture capital firm. See also the National Venture Capital Association (NVCA). The best strategy is to know your industry and do the research to learn about the VC firms that boosted companies 6 to 8 years older than yours. Then, contact the VC firm to find out how and when you can pitch to them.

Depending on your community, there are angel investor groups all over the country. These are smaller investors with substantial money to invest in good business ideas. The amount of money raised is usually less than one would receive from a VC firm, and the management insider skills may be less but still very good with the angel investor.

The best bet for you is to find venture capital with a firm that knows your industry. They will know the vendors and the customers and provide you with valuable information that would take you hours, maybe years, to obtain. It's back to networking; you will be plugged into the VC firms' network, and then you will be introduced to powerful companies and people who can help your company grow.

It is most important to be prepared, explain your product, know the numbers exactly, and not present pie-in-the-sky estimates or wild forecasts and predictions. You have to present sold ideas and solid numbers. Also, the IP, intellectual property you will want to have in hand copyrights, patents, trademarks, and other intellectual property, this should

Financing, Venture Capital And Private Equity / 233

all be done, finished, and complete. You have to be a good communicator, a sharp presenter, and know and explain your management team and present any applicable letters of commitment from people that will help manage the company. The business plan and the explanation of how you will execute the plan with precision are a must. Explain how your company is poised for substantial and rapid growth.

Last but not least is crowdfunding. This is popular for smaller companies. Many small business that are now medium-sized private companies got their start through a polished plea for crowdfunding.

Crowdfunding is relatively new and was a way for the SEC to turn a blind eye to people looking for smaller amounts of capital. Much of this was sought before there were organized online crowdfunding sites. People would offer partnership interests in their business if they would put in capital to get the business started. You have to be careful how you do this so that you do not run afoul of well-established Federal and state laws about investment offerings.

Crowdfunding is a financing method that raises money by soliciting small individual investments or contributions from a large number of people. It is a popular way to raise funds for a range of artistic, humanitarian, or social causes. Donation based or reward based crowdfunding models like GoFundMe or Kickstarter do not provide a financial return.

All equity based crowdfunding platforms, which raise capital for startups and larger companies, are designed to provide investors with a financial return.

Crowdfunding provides an exemption from the registration requirements for securities based crowdfunding, allowing companies to offer and sell up to $5 million of their securities without having to register the offering with the SEC.

There are several how to books about crowdfunding. There are many consultants who, for a fee, will align your pitch to fit a niche that they know will work to raise capital.

There are four kinds of crowdfunding campaigns you can use for your business. With donation based funding, contributors give money without receiving anything in return. In equity funding, backers get shares of the business. For debt based funding, donors are repaid with interest.

There are many choices when it comes to crowdfunding. You have to analyze your offering. Is it a plea for help? There are certain funds that serve well favored industries. You don't want to pursue crowdfunding for manufacturing on a site that favors the hospitality industry. Know what you are doing and what site best favors your position. A good story and a plea for help have launched many good companies that are running solidly today.

Once again, the SBA is also there to help small and medium-sized businesses with guaranteed Federally backed loans.

To launch or take a business to the next level, access to capital is a very important step for the business owner to know, research, and be aware of. Larger bank back rooms also know where investment capital is and how to reach it.

A small business can gain access to capital for growth and survival through various sources. Here are some common options:

1. **Traditional Bank Loans:** Small businesses can apply for loans from commercial banks. These loans may require collateral, a strong credit history, and a detailed business plan or loan proposal. Banks offer different types of loans, such as term loans, lines of credit, and Small Business Administration (SBA) loans.

2. **Small Business Administration (SBA) Loans:** The U.S. Small Business Administration offers loan programs specifically designed for small businesses. SBA loans generally have more flexible terms and lower interest rates than traditional bank loans. The most popular program is the SBA 7(a) loan, which can be used for various business purposes. The business plan and the SBA application have to have substance, maybe highlighting that the business is minority owned, the business will bring jobs to the city in which the business is located, necessary to pump up the local economy. These pleas that hit the sweet spot with SBA may give you a competitive advantage in getting the loan. SBA is known to seek collateral; they want to see that you have skin in the game!

3. **Microloans:** Microloan programs are offered by nonprofit organizations and community lenders. They provide small amounts of capital to entrepreneurs and small businesses that might not qualify for traditional bank loans. Microloans typically have shorter terms and lower loan amounts.

4. **Online Lenders:** Online lending platforms have gained popularity in recent years. These platforms provide loans to small businesses with a streamlined application process. They often have less stringent requirements than traditional banks but may have higher interest rates. Know in advance they will want to see your bank statements for 90 to 180 days to measure your monthly deposits. They may also want to see current financial statements for you and the business. They sometimes have reduced rates for borrowers who have collateral.

5. **Crowdfunding:** Crowdfunding platforms, such as Kickstarter and Indiegogo, allow businesses to raise funds from a large number of individuals who contribute small amounts. This can be an effective way to generate capital while also creating buzz and at-

tracting customers. You will want to work hard to convert your crowdfunding doner into a business customer.

6. **Angel Investors:** Angel investors are individuals who invest their personal funds in early-stage businesses in exchange for equity ownership. They often provide not only capital but also expertise, mentorship, and networking opportunities. They may have valuable local knowledge that will help the business.

7. **Venture Capital:** Venture capital firms invest in high-growth potential startups and businesses in exchange for equity. While venture capital is more common for tech startups, certain industries and businesses with significant growth potential can attract venture capital funding.

8. **Grants:** Some organizations, private foundations, and government agencies offer grants to small businesses, especially those engaged in research, development, or socially impactful initiatives. These grants do not need to be repaid, but the application process can be competitive.

9. **Friends and Family:** Small businesses can seek capital from friends, family members, or personal connections who believe in the business or believe in you and are thus willing to invest. Formalizing these arrangements through legal documentation is essential to protect both parties.

10. **Trade Credit and Supplier Financing:** Building good relationships with suppliers can lead to trade credit, allowing businesses to obtain goods and services on credit terms. Some suppliers may offer financing options to help small businesses manage their cash flow.

11. **Mature Company Investment:** McDonald's, Panda, and a host of other restaurants have invested in new restaurant start-ups that show promise in being able to grow and expand. Direct other company investment may be available to you, but you have to lay out the benefits and make a professional, polished plea for the funds. This happens in manufacturing and other industries as well. Seek out mature companies or suppliers that will benefit from your growth.

Remember that the availability of these options may vary based on your location, industry, and business stage. It's important to thoroughly research each option, consider the terms and requirements, and choose the one that best aligns with your business needs and goals. Consulting with a financial advisor or small business development center can provide valuable guidance.

Without access to capital, businesses will struggle to expand their operations, upgrade equipment, and hire additional employees. Access to capital is particularly important for small businesses that often lack financial resources. Most people need to access capital when starting or growing a business.

The inability to get funding will inhibit your business's ability to purchase assets and resources needed for expansion. Lack of capital may also jeopardize your ability to cover your day-to-day operational expenses. Rent, salaries, insurance, all these things cost money on an ongoing basis.

Therefore, small and medium-sized businesses have to have a friendly relationship with a banker, hopefully, the bank manager or president. Having a line of credit can be helpful to a business owner to enable continued growth and expansion of the business or to cover unexpected costs.

Access to capital is crucial for the growth and success of small and medium-sized businesses. It serves as the lifeblood that fuels their operations, enables expansion, and empowers innovation. Here are the key reasons why capital is essential for small and medium-sized businesses.

Capital is often required to establish a new small and medium-sized business (SMB). It covers initial expenses like equipment, inventory, marketing, and overhead costs. Many startups struggle to launch or sustain their operations without access to capital, leading to a high failure rate.

SMBs with access to capital can seize growth opportunities and expand their operations. Whether it's opening new locations, investing in technology and infrastructure, or hiring additional employees, capital allows SMBs to scale their business and increase their market share.

In a rapidly evolving business landscape, SMBs need capital to innovate and stay competitive. Investment in research and development, product diversification, and technology adoption enables SMBs to adapt to changing market trends, customer demands, and industry disruptions.

Effective marketing is essential for SMBs to attract customers and build brand recognition. Capital helps fund marketing campaigns, advertising, social media presence, and other promotional activities that enhance visibility and customer engagement.

Capital enables SMBs to recruit and retain talented employees. It covers salaries, training programs, employee benefits, and incentives that foster a skilled and motivated workforce. Investing in human capital enhances productivity and customer service, contributing to long-term success.

SMBs face various risks, such as economic downturns, supply chain disruptions, or unexpected expenses. Access to capital provides a safety net, allowing businesses to weather challenging times, cover unforeseen costs, and maintain stability during periods of uncertainty.

Access to capital is vital for SMBs at every stage of their journey. It fuels their growth, drives innovation, supports marketing efforts, fosters a talented workforce, and helps manage risks. Governments, financial institutions, and investors play a crucial role in facilitating capital access for SMBs, as it contributes to economic growth, job creation, and overall prosperity.

**CHAPTER 13**

# The Pursuit of Profit

You have to develop a mindset to achieve profit. You cannot get so tied up in making the product that you forget that the focus, objective and a keeping the business alive necessity, is to earn a profit. You have a duty to yourself, your family, your ego, your banker, and your customers to operate the business in an organized, efficient, and effective way so as to end up at the end of the quarter and the end of the year by hitting your well-established profit target.

To get to profit, it's back to the accounting class:

**Sales minus Cost of Sales equals Gross Profit...**

Gross Profit

Less:

General and administrative costs

Depreciation

Income taxes

Then equals… Net Profit…

You have to memorize and indelibly sear into the brain the formula, the recipe, to achieve a profit. Your focus has to be aimed at making your "net profit target." The target can be stated as either an amount or as a percentage.

If you do not have the net profit target amount in mind at the beginning of the month, it is unlikely that you will achieve the profit target at the end of the month.

The gross profit tells analysts how well you did in making the product or service. In some businesses, it is the measure of how well the factory made the product. In other businesses, it is how well the construction went in the field. In growing grapes, it is how well it went in growing, watering, and harvesting. The product in a law firm, the gross profit reveals how well the time was spent doing the client work and if a lot of time was unbillable, thus causing the gross profit to be lower.

The net profit is arrived at by starting with gross profit and then subtracting overhead costs:

Rent, utilities, supplies, office expenses, insurance, repairs, travel, Continuing education, postage, bank fees, computer paper, janitorial services

Legal fees, accounting fees, consulting fees, interest expense

Depreciation and income tax costs

The bottom line of all of this is, the business, net profit. The metric by which all entrepreneurs are judged.

To achieve greater net profit, you will need to know your industry.

You have to, in your "spare time," do research to first see how to make your product better and then widening your sights into keeping in touch with what is happening in your industry.

Belong and become part of the leadership in your industry. You will become exposed to things that you never would have considered or thought of when sitting in your office. Lean toward being the top, the best in your industry.

If you join in, do the work in your industry, and operate your business as a shining example, you will soon become recognized by your industry. Industry recognition is a great way to ignite sales and give a reason for the public relations function to get your name in the media and earn millions of dollars worth of free advertising.

Joining the industry and becoming involved in state or national organizations is helpful and rewarding. The chief reason to do this is that along the way, you learn things about the industry that help your business dominate the industry and move your products up higher in customer recognition and acceptance. You want to be the person from Harvard University who knows more than anyone else in all facets of your business and your industry. Don't just participate in the game. Become the best.

I want to emphasize the vital importance of profit in any entrepreneurial business. Profitability is the lifeblood that fuels growth, innovation, and sustainability. It enables you to invest in your people, expand your operations, and create value for your customers and shareholders. Here's why profit is crucial:

Profit ensures the survival of your business. Without a healthy bottom line, you cannot cover your expenses, pay your employees, or reinvest in your company's future. Profitability provides a solid foundation upon which you can build and weather economic uncertainties.

Profit allows you to attract and retain top talent. It enables you to offer competitive salaries, benefits, and growth opportunities to your employees. A motivated and skilled workforce is essential for driving innovation, improving productivity, and delivering exceptional products and services to your customers.

Profitability also empowers you to invest in research and development, technological advancements, and market expansion. These investments fuel your ability to stay ahead of the competition, adapt to changing customer needs, and seize new opportunities. They enable you to develop cutting-edge products, improve operational efficiency, and explore new markets, thus driving growth and market leadership.

Additionally, profit ensures stability and resilience during challenging times. It allows you to build financial reserves, which act as a safety net in the face of unforeseen circumstances or economic downturns. Many businesses have tax incentives for investing their cash reserves and for creating retirement accounts. This resilience enables you to sustain your operations, support your employees, and continue serving your customers even during difficult periods.

Profit is not just a number on a profit and loss report; it is the life force that propels entrepreneurial businesses forward. Profit enables you to invest, innovate, and create value for all stakeholders. You should remain committed to driving profitability while upholding your values, fostering a positive work culture, and delivering exceptional results. Together, you can continue to build a successful and sustainable future.

Learn along the way, gain keen insight, and then do outside research on your own to become the best, the best there is, the best there was, the best that will ever be.

The structure and the components of profit. The calculation of profit is not the feeling you have at the end of a month, the feeling that you did well. Profit is an accounting function that accurately matches the sales for the month with all the related subtractions or costs of making those goods or services. Each month, the accountants can figure out what the sales are for the month. From this, the goods that were returned are next subtracted.

Next is the calculation of the "cost of goods sold." In general, this is the raw materials and the labor that went into making the goods or services for the month.

Raw materials, subcontractors, assemblies, fasteners, containers, packaging materials, and shipping crates. Then, the production requirements may entail some laboratory personnel and lab supplies, engineers, and quality control efforts.

There is a gathering of all the costs that went directly into making the product or service.

Then comes the drum roll: after you do the math and subtract the production costs from net sales, you arrive at a gross profit. Gross profit, knowing this number, is knowing the pulse of the business organism.

As a CEO, gross profit is an extremely crucial metric for assessing the financial health and overall performance of a company. Gross profit represents the revenue generated from the sale of goods or services minus the direct costs associated with producing or delivering those goods or services. It provides valuable insights into the efficiency and effectiveness of a company's core operations.

Gross profit is a direct indicator of how well a company's core operations are performing. By deducting the cost of goods sold (COGS) from revenue, gross profit reveals the profitability of producing the products or services a company offers. It allows CEOs to understand whether their pricing strategies, production processes, and supply chain management are generating profits or facing challenges.

Cost Management: Analyzing the gross profit margin (gross profit divided by revenue) provides insights into a company's ability to control costs. If the margin, expressed as a percentage, is shrinking over time, it may indicate increasing production costs, inefficient procurement, or pricing pressures. Conversely, an expanding margin suggests effective cost management in producing the product and speaks volumes about your pricing strategy.

Gross profit analysis helps assess a company's competitiveness within its industry. By comparing gross profit margins with industry peers or known industry standards, CEOs can determine if their pricing strategies are competitive and whether their cost structures are efficient. A consistently lower gross profit margin than competitors may indicate the need to address cost inefficiencies or explore new revenue streams or product price increases.

Growth Potential: Gross profit is vital for evaluating a company's growth prospects. A healthy gross profit margin provides the financial foundation to invest in research and development, marketing, and expansion. Investors and analysts often use gross profit trends to gauge the company's ability to fund future initiatives, repay debt, and generate sustainable long-term growth.

Gross profit is a key metric for investors and analysts when assessing a company's financial health. It provides insights into a company's ability to generate profits before considering other expenses like operating costs, taxes, and interest. A strong gross profit performance instills confidence in stakeholders and can positively impact a company's stock price and market perception.

From a CEO's perspective, gross profit is a critical measure that reflects a company's core profitability, cost management abilities, competitive positioning, and growth potential and influences investor confidence. It provides a comprehensive view of the company's financial health and serves as a vital tool for decision making and strategic planning.

Pay close attention to the importance of knowing your gross profit percentage, as this will be an indicator of how efficient the production area of the company is.

This concept applies to all businesses: doctor's offices, dental offices, law firms, car repair garages, restaurants, hotels, golf courses, bowling alleys, grape growers, wineries, and the list goes on.

After the gross profit calculation, the accountants will add all the other business operations costs, such as overhead costs, general and administrative costs, research and development costs, depreciation allocation for the period, interest expense, and income tax costs.

The depreciation allocation is often confusing to people. If you have a piece of equipment and it is projected to wear out in six years, it costs $250,000 to purchase. Then, the depreciation allocation for each year is going to be $41,667 per year. The cost of using that piece of equipment for the production floor is going to be his allocated cost of $41,667 each year or $3,472 per month. To run a business, you have to know these things.

To arrive at what is the profit for this particular period, the math continues. From gross profit, certain other expenses in operating the business are going to be considered. This takes into consideration each check that left the company's checkbook and the unpaid invoices/costs at the end of the year. The accountant's idea is to gather all of the costs attributed to the year unpaid or not. They try to achieve the result of taking the sales and matching all of the costs for the year in making those sales and listing these amounts on the Profit and Loss report for the year, perfectly matching the sales and the costs of operating the business during the period of making those sales.

From gross profit will be subtracted the general and administrative expenses, such things as:

1. **Operating Expenses:** These are the indirect costs incurred in running the business operations and include items such as non-production salaries and wages, rent, utilities, marketing expenses, research, insurance and development costs, and administrative expenses. Operating expenses are subtracted from the gross profit to calculate the operating net profit.

2. **Depreciation and Amortization:** companies often have significant investments in machinery, equipment, and other fixed assets. Accountants allocate the cost of these assets over their useful lives through depreciation and amortization expenses. These expenses are subtracted from the gross profit to derive the operating net income.

3. **Interest Expenses:** If the company has taken on debt, interest expenses on loans and credit facilities are deducted from the operating income.

4. **Taxes:** The income tax expense is calculated based on the company's taxable income, taking into account applicable tax laws and regulations.

After deducting all these costs, the remaining amount is the net profit, which represents the final profitability of the company after accounting for all expenses incurred in the production and operation processes.

Net profit is a measure of the company's financial health and stability. It indicates that the business is generating more revenue than expenses, resulting in positive profitability. A healthy net profit demonstrates that the company has sufficient funds to cover its operating costs, debt obligations, and funds to reinvest in growth opportunities. This financial stability helps the company weather economic downturns, market fluctuations, and unexpected expenses. Having a profit allows the company to put money into a long-term savings account or an investment account to preserve the company's longevity.

Profitability is a key driver of sustainable operations and growth. By generating consistent net profits, an entrepreneurial enterprise can reinvest those earnings into expanding operations, developing new products or services, improving infrastructure, hiring talent, or pursuing market opportunities. This reinvestment fuels business growth and helps the company remain competitive in the long run.

Investor and Creditor Confidence: A company that consistently demonstrates healthy net profits is more likely to attract investors and creditors. Investors seek businesses that can provide a return on their investment, while creditors want assurance that the company can repay its debts. Positive net profits are an indication of the company's ability to generate returns and repay borrowed funds. This confidence helps raise capital, secure loans, and build strong relationships with stakeholders.

Profitability acts as a buffer against risks and uncertainties. It provides the company with financial resources to withstand unexpected challenges, such as market downturns, regulatory changes, or unforeseen expenses. When a company faces difficulties, a healthy net profit allows for strategic decisions, such as cost cutting measures, diversification efforts, or investments in innovation, which can help navigate through tough times and protect the company's longevity. Profits can be held in savings accounts to protect the company from any challenges that present themselves.

Net profit is a crucial factor in determining the value of a company. When evaluating a company for acquisition or merger, potential buyers or partners often consider the company's profitability as a key metric. A consistently profitable enterprise is more likely to command a higher valuation, which benefits the founders, shareholders, and other stakeholders.

A healthy net profit is vital for the longevity of an entrepreneurial enterprise as it ensures financial stability, supports sustainable growth, instills confidence in investors and creditors, mitigates risks, and enhances the company's overall value. By consistently generating profits, the company can secure its future, reinvest in its operations, and adapt to changing market conditions, ultimately protecting its long-term success.

When a business, no matter how large or how small, there is no assurance that the company next year will earn a profit. There are a number of external factors which might disturb profitability. Economic downturns may make consumer disposable income disappear; therefore, the demand for your product or service will go down while your costs stay the same or similar. When consumer demand goes down, that means fewer of your customers are going to order your product, which will reduce your sales while all your costs stay the same. This may cause your profitable company of five years to suffer a net loss from operations in year six.

The US economy has not remained the same over the last 100 years. We can chart through the years and prepare a graph to show there were periods of uptrends, some flat periods, and periods of economic downturns.

This intensifies the need for a company to stash some cash in a rainy day fund to help the company through periods of economic downturn.

There are several external factors that can cause a profitable company in the US to suddenly incur a loss from operations. Here are some possible examples:

During an economic recession or downturn, consumer spending tends to decrease, impacting a company's sales and revenue. Reduced demand for products or services can lead to a decline in profitability and the showing of operating losses.

Shifts in market dynamics, such as increased competition, changing customer preferences, or disruptive technologies, can negatively affect a company's profitability. If a company fails to adapt to these changes or loses its competitive edge, it may experience a decline in sales and incur operational losses. Many large US companies went out of business because they did not keep up, adapt, and change with the times.

Changes in government regulations, such as new laws or stricter compliance requirements, can impose additional costs on businesses. For example, increased taxes, tariffs, or regulatory fees can reduce profit margins and lead to operational losses. Fees, fines, or penalties can also deliver a blow to profitability.

Natural Disasters or Unforeseen Events: Events like natural disasters, pandemics, or geopolitical instability can disrupt supply chains, hinder production, or impact customer demand. These unexpected events can result in operational challenges, increased costs, and revenue loss, leading to overall losses. Some everyday occurrences, such as fire, flood, earthquake, or damaging weather related conditions, can affect your business.

Currency Fluctuations: Companies engaged in international trade can be affected by currency fluctuations. If a company's domestic currency strengthens against other currencies, its exports may become more expensive, leading to a decline in sales and profitability. International business has a lot of exposure to conditions that may change quickly that would disrupt profitability. Doing business in a communist-run country comes with its own set of problems.

Dependence on specific suppliers or vendors can pose risks to a company's operations. If a critical supplier faces disruptions, such as bankruptcy, production delays, or quality issues, it can impact the company's ability to deliver products or services, leading to losses.

Changes in Labor Costs: Significant increases in labor costs, such as minimum wage hikes, worker strikes or changes in labor laws, can impact a company's profitability. Higher wages or increased employee benefit expenses can squeeze profit margins and result in operating losses.

It's important to note that the impact of these external factors can vary depending on the industry, company size, and specific circumstances. Companies often employ risk management strategies and contingency plans to mitigate the effects of such external factors and maintain profitability. Properly forecasting danger ahead will cause people within the company to react to keep problems away and the supply chain humming.

## CHAPTER 14

# How to Start Your Business

Before you begin your business, you need to have a business plan. A business plan lays out any objectives you have as well as your strategy for achieving those objectives. This plan is important for getting investors on board, as well as measuring how successful your business is.

The business plan is the starting road map, enabling you to stay on the road, and contains metrics to measure the business's growth and development. It is useful to break the entrepreneurial process into five phases:

- Idea generation
- Opportunity evaluation
- Planning

- Company formation/launch
- Growth

The entrepreneurial process can be thought of as a five-phase journey, each phase building upon the previous, ultimately leading to the growth of a thriving enterprise.

The first phase is idea generation, where the entrepreneur's creativity flourishes, giving birth to innovative concepts. It involves identifying problems, recognizing market gaps, and brainstorming novel solutions. Here, inspiration and ideation reign supreme.

Moving forward, the second phase encompasses opportunity evaluation. It's crucial to conduct comprehensive market research, assess competition, and analyze the viability and scalability of the ideas generated. This phase involves meticulous evaluation and validation, allowing entrepreneurs to make informed decisions about the potential for success. This is where you identify and choose a business you want to be in. From teaching yoga to performing brain surgery, you have to take a look at the universe, understand what you enjoy doing and sharing or helping others with. Then where the dart hits the board is the business you are going to prepare to launch. Choose wisely and choose a business with a good profit margin!

Once a promising opportunity is identified, the third phase begins: planning. Entrepreneurs craft a robust business plan in this stage, outlining key strategies, operational processes, and financial projections. Thorough planning is essential for securing resources, attracting investors, and ensuring a solid foundation for future growth.

The fourth phase entails company formation and launch. Entrepreneurs must navigate legal requirements, register their businesses, obtain all necessary permissions, permits, and employer identification numbers, and assemble a capable team of talented people. Effective execution of the business plan is paramount, as this phase marks the birth of the venture and its entry into the market. You want to project confidence that your team is capable of quick execution and is up for the challenge.

The fifth phase encompasses growth, where the entrepreneur strives to scale their business. This involves implementing marketing strategies, refining operations, and constantly innovating or simply improving the product to better meet customer needs. The growth phase is marked by continuous adaptation and expansion, creating a sustainable and thriving enterprise.

Know that the entrepreneurial process is a dynamic journey consisting of idea generation, opportunity evaluation, planning, company formation/launch, and growth. Each phase plays a vital role in shaping the trajectory and success of the venture, requiring determination, dedication, resilience, and a visionary mindset. So, embrace the entrepreneurial spirit and embark on this transformative path with passion and purpose.

In order to start your business, you need to consider these important points.

Search or attend an entrepreneurial brainstorming class to put your finger on exactly what you are going to pursue. It may be that you found your passion and your heart's desire in what business you are going to start.

Conduct market research for market research will tell you if there's an opportunity to turn your idea into a successful business. It's a way to gather information about potential customers and businesses already operating in your area. Use that information to find a competitive advantage for your business.

Choose a business name. It's not easy to pick the perfect name. You'll want one that reflects your brand and captures your spirit. You'll also want to make sure your business name isn't already being used by someone else. You may want to protect your business name with a trademark. Be clever, have fun, and choose a name that will be easy for the customer to remember in your quest to have your product or service become a household name.

Know that Coke, Kleenex, Google, Tesla, bubble wrap, and Thermos are all meaningless words at their origin, but by building the brand, they are now household words.

Investigate the types of legal entities that are available and affordably by you. Remember that tax savings, legal reasons, estate planning and asset protection are key reasons people operate their business in the corporate or LLC format.

Once you have chosen the entity type and selected a business name, open a bank account in the name of the business. This is a very important step.

Do business with a bank that will, in the future, be able to offer you a business line of credit. Go meet the manager and do business with someone who clicks with you. Make this person your friend. Learn what it takes to become a member of the private banking department of your bank. Get the bank manager on your team and make them aware of the product or service that you will sell. Begin to develop an important relationship with the banker for your business. Decide at what level two signatures are required on a check before it can be issued. Some businesses require two signatures of owners if the amount of the check is over $5,000.

Register with Federal and State agencies to obtain business employer identification numbers and become prepared once you have employees to comply with labor laws and proper reporting to Federal and state agencies on a quarterly basis to comply with payroll tax matters.

Be aware of any licenses or permits you may need to operate your business. Make the proper application and keep the documents in a safe place or display them if necessary. Be aware of the renewal process and mark a calendar to renew the license or permit.

Choose a business location. Your business location is one of the most important decisions you'll make. Whether setting up a brick and mortar business or launching an online store, your choices could affect your taxes, legal requirements, and revenue. In choosing a location, know that many businesses are located near where the raw materials are made. You will want to consider your target market and the customers you will sell to and use demographic studies to locate your business in the best location available to attract and service your customer's needs.

Suppose the location choice involves negotiating a long-term lease. You may want a lease that does not have every year increases as, quite likely, you cannot raise your prices on a yearly basis to be able to afford increased rent. The lease may contain options for you to renew the lease if you choose to do so. So careful thought needs to go into the lease to protect the long-term existence of your business. This is so important, and many entrepreneurs forget to protect their future by negotiating and securing a long-term lease. The other part of this is demographics and sometimes logistics. You have to locate the business where it is easy for your customers to come to you.

This is an exact science that needs to be figured out with careful studies of car traffic, foot traffic, and other components identifying how customers are going to enter your location. The opposition here is the commercial landlord. You will have to charm them and help them understand the economics of your business will not allow for constant rent increases.

A whole book can be written on the tales of entrepreneurs and their landlords. The initial McDonald's model was to buy the real estate, securing their future in a well-researched location. Most entrepreneurs don't have room for a big down payment and must rent the location. When renting, be sure that you are sure of the habits of your target market of customers. The landlord is responsible in a shopping center for delivering foot traffic; be sure the landlord intends to do this to help make your business successful.

Consider joining a business organization that will help you with networking and spreading the word about your business opening.

Get in touch with your determination. Be prepared for whatever curve ball comes toward you as you begin to grow and develop your business while falling back on your entrepreneurial mindset. Stay the course, do not become complacent, drive forward, create sales, control your costs, and enjoy the stress relief when you earn a profit.

The entrepreneurial mindset is characterized by a combination of vision, resilience, determination, creativity, and risk-taking. Entrepreneurs possess a clear vision of their goals and are driven by a passion to bring their ideas to life.

They embrace challenges and view the small failures as opportunities for learning and growth. With a creative mindset, entrepreneurs constantly seek innovative solutions, and they adapt to changing circumstances.

Remember, you are the captain of the ship. You are in charge of the direction you take to start your business. You have to steer the ship in the right direction. Become in charge.

Entrepreneurs are willing to take calculated risks and make tough decisions, understanding that success often requires stepping outside of their comfort zone. They are self-motivated persistent, and maintain a positive attitude, fueling their determination to overcome obstacles and achieve their business goals.

The steps to remember for the new entrepreneur in starting a new business:

Starting a new business requires careful planning and execution to increase the chances of success.

Idea Generation: identify a viable business idea that aligns with your passion, skills, and market demand. Conduct thorough market research to validate your concept. Hatching a good idea for some is difficult. This must be accomplished so that you know what direction to go next. There are many resources available to help you create the business idea that you want to pursue.

Business Plan: Create a comprehensive business plan that outlines your goals, target market, competition analysis, marketing strategies, financial projections, and operational details. This is an important part so you can come out of the starting gate like a racehorse or an Olympic athlete leaving the starting blocks in a 200-meter race.

Here is a jingle that I created for an entrepreneurship class. Though it refers to a man, you can use this jingle and substitute he, she, or gender neutral. It's a jingle for your office wall!

> "A man without a plan is lost, oh dear,
>
> But fear not, there's a solution that's clear!
>
> With determination, he'll find his way,
>
> Charting a course for a brighter day!
>
> He'll dream big and set goals in his sight,
>
> Taking action with all of his might.
>
> No hurdle too high, no challenge too grand,

He'll navigate life with a steadfast hand.

With a plan in hand, he'll thrive and succeed,

Unlocking potential with each noble deed.

So, embrace the power of planning, my friend,

And watch your dreams soar and never end!

For a man with a plan can truly find,

The path to greatness, one step at a time.

So, seize the moment, ignite your fire,

And let your dreams soar higher and higher!"

Next on the list of what to consider are the legal and accounting issues. You should seek the guidance of the appropriate professionals to help you get your business properly formed in a tax-free manner, with maximum asset protection in place.

These professionals can share guidance on what a start-up enterprise should consider. If you are purchasing a business, these professionals can help you with your due diligence in investigating the business before you purchase it.

My preference in the matter is to seek out a competent management consulting firm that, over and over again, has a track record of helping and launching new businesses. Here, you will meet professionals that focus on operations and focus on success. They can provide you with guidance because this is their business, and they do this all day, every day for years and years, and bring to the table a lot of practical experience.

In today's dynamic business landscape, entrepreneurs require expert guidance to navigate challenges and seize opportunities. While law firms and accounting firms play crucial roles in servicing and supporting business operations from a distance, management consultants offer a unique perspective and an array of strategic tools that can provide entrepreneurs with superior guidance. Let's explore the reasons why management consultants are often better suited to assist entrepreneurs compared to law firms or accounting firms.

## Holistic Business Perspective:

Management consultants specialize in analyzing the overall business ecosystem, encompassing market dynamics, industry trends, and competitive landscapes. Their ability to assess the broader context enables them to offer entrepreneurs a holistic perspective on their venture. This broad understanding goes beyond legal or financial aspects and allows consultants to provide strategic guidance aligned with the company's long-term goals.

## Strategic Planning and Execution:

While law firms and accounting firms typically focus on legal compliance and financial reporting, management consultants excel in strategic planning and execution with precision. They help entrepreneurs set clear objectives, develop robust business strategies, and execute them effectively. Management Consultants can offer valuable insights on market entry strategies, product development, organizational design, and operational efficiency, enabling entrepreneurs to make informed decisions to drive growth and profitability.

## Innovation and Adaptability:

The rapidly evolving business landscape demands constant innovation and adaptability. Management consultants bring fresh perspectives and best practices from various industries, allowing entrepreneurs to stay ahead of the curve. They can assist in identifying emerging trends in new technology, leveraging disruptive technologies, and implementing agile methodologies. By fostering a culture of innovation, management consultants help entrepreneurs remain competitive in an ever changing market.

Here is why a management consulting firm can provide you with better guidance than a law firm or accounting firm.

Entrepreneurs often face significant challenges when implementing organizational changes or undertaking business transformations. Management consultants specialize in change management, offering expertise in managing transitions, minimizing disruptions, and aligning stakeholders' interests. Their structured approach, combined with experience in managing complex projects, ensures that entrepreneurs can navigate change successfully and achieve desired outcomes.

## Customized Solutions:

Management consultants provide tailored solutions based on an in-depth understanding of the entrepreneur's unique needs and business goals. They go beyond standard templates and provide customized strategies and recommendations that address specific challenges. Consultants work closely with entrepreneurs, collaborating on every step of the journey, ensuring that solutions are practical, implementable, and aligned with the entrepreneur's vision.

Many private equity firms and some banks require the business owner to engage a management consulting firm familiar with their industry before funding occurs.

While law firms and accounting firms provide indispensable helpful services, management consultants work closer to business operations and the front lines; through careful, useful analysis, they offer a comprehensive and strategic approach to support entrepreneurs. Management consultants are involved with daily business operations. When consultants do this year in and year out for 20 years, they gather a library of knowledge that can help you navigate daily, monthly, and quarterly through any challenges that present themselves.

Their ability to provide organic, holistic, useful perspectives, strategic planning expertise, innovation driven guidance, change management capabilities, and customized solutions make them valuable partners for entrepreneurs seeking sustainable growth and competitive advantage. The management consulting firm has at its disposal industry experts that can shed light on your specific business or business bottleneck.

By leveraging the diverse and well-honed skill set of management consultants, entrepreneurs can unlock their full potential and navigate the complex business landscape with confidence. If success is important, engage a management consulting firm to assist you with getting on course and pointed in the right direction. Mature companies hire management consultants to get their sales unstuck and onto a trajectory of sales growth and earnings improvement.

In starting your business, you need to consider the legal structure of the business and map out an organizational chart when necessary.

Legal Structure: Choose an appropriate legal structure for your business, such as sole proprietorship, partnership, or limited liability company (LLC). Consult with legal, tax and financial professionals to understand the implications of each structure.

To properly form your company, you need the help of good professionals who know your industry. The legal structure has financial planning, tax planning, asset protection, succession planning, and estate planning implications.

Your choice of entity is very important. It is possible to start with one type of entity, and as the business grows, you may want to transition into a different kind of entity. Bear in mind that legal protection, liability protection, asset protection, and tax planning are things that must be considered when starting out and selecting a business entity.

Financing: Determine how you will fund your business. Explore options like personal savings, credit cards, loans, grants, family, friends, venture capital, private equity, or investors. Develop a financial plan to estimate your startup costs and ongoing expenses. Create a semiannual budget. Once underway, establish a savings program so that you can stash some cash away for entrepreneurial bumps in the road, unexpected events, or downturns in the national economy. Having some extra cash can keep your business afloat during challenging times or growth spurts.

Branding and Marketing: Develop a strong brand identity, including a memorable name, logo, and website. Create a marketing plan to promote your products or services effectively. Leverage social media, digital advertising, and traditional marketing techniques.

Branding holds immense significance for a startup entrepreneurial company. In a crowded marketplace, a strong brand becomes a powerful differentiator. It embodies the company's unique identity, values, and vision, establishing an emotional connection with customers.

A well-crafted brand instills trust, credibility, and loyalty, setting the stage for long-term success. It helps the company stand out from competitors, making it memorable and recognizable. A compelling brand attracts investors, partners, and top talent, which are important factors in enhancing the company's growth prospects. It simplifies decision making for customers and boosts their confidence in the company's offerings.

Branding is the foundation upon which a startup can build its reputation, expand its customer base, and ultimately thrive in a dynamic business landscape. You want your brand to stand for quality, so you need to be sure that you deliver a quality product or service.

Operations and Infrastructure: Establish your physical or virtual location, procure necessary equipment or technology, and set up essential systems for accounting, inventory management, and customer relationship management. Operations and producing the product are very important. Think through how you are going to receive the raw material. How are you going to plan and set up the tenant improvements to conduct high speed production? How are you going to ship the product to your customers?

If you have a physical location, the lease is an important part of setting up your business. You will want to be able to and have the right to occupy the building for a long time. If you don't want a one-year lease, find out how much joy landlords take in socking it to you with rent increases. Work out all of the details and the increases at the outset. A five-year lease with four five-year options and minimal rent increases is optimal. If you hunt, you can find a building that has been vacant for a long time. Then you are in a better position to pay a flat rent over the long term.

Talented Team: How are you going to attract top talent to your company? What technology are you going to use? Is there electrical capacity in place to run your business productively?

Setting up operations and infrastructure correctly is paramount for any new entrepreneurial business. It lays the foundation for long-term success and ensures smooth functioning from the outset.

Considering and establishing efficient operations enables streamlined processes and maximizes productivity. Careful planning and implementation of standard operating procedures ensure that tasks are executed effectively, reducing errors and optimizing resource allocation. This, in turn, enhances customer satisfaction, as timely and reliable delivery becomes a hallmark of the business.

A solid infrastructure provides the backbone for growth and scalability. Investing in robust technology, equipment, and facilities enables seamless operations and facilitates expansion. A well designed and plumbed IT network, secure data management systems, and appropriate physical infrastructure foster innovation, collaboration, and adaptability, allowing the business to meet evolving market demands.

Moreover, setting up operations and infrastructure correctly promotes cost effectiveness. Careful analysis of business requirements helps identify essential resources and eliminate unnecessary expenses. Optimal inventory management, efficient supply chain logistics, and strategic vendor partnerships reduce overheads and enhance profitability, ultimately contributing to the business's financial health.

A strong operational foundation fosters a positive work environment. Well defined roles and responsibilities, coupled with effective communication channels, promote clarity and teamwork. When employees have the necessary tools and resources, their morale improves, leading to higher job satisfaction, increased productivity, and lower turnover rates.

Correctly setting up operations and infrastructure instills confidence in stakeholders, such as investors, bankers, lenders, and partners. A well organized business inspires trust and demonstrates professionalism, enhancing the likelihood of securing funding and attracting valuable collaborations.

The importance of correctly setting up operations and infrastructure for a new entrepreneurial business cannot be overstated. It optimizes productivity, enables growth and scalability, reduces costs, fosters a positive work environment, and instills confidence in stakeholders. Entrepreneurs lay the groundwork for a successful and sustainable venture by investing time and effort in these foundational aspects.

Negotiation Skills: Some businesses launch easily, and some don't. As an entrepreneur, you are going to need to understand and deal with conflict. Conflict in a business is inevitable. Conflict may erupt with the postal carrier, a key vendor, an employee, a notice from your law firm that you are being sued by your former roommate, and the list goes on. You have to develop skills to resolve conflict.

One of the skills you need to have in the bag is good negotiating skills. There are many classes that you can take about negotiating. Some are from the legal point of view, and some are from psychology. Here are some ideas to keep in mind when developing your negotiating strategy and style.

Active Listening: Active listening involves paying close attention to the other party's words, non-verbal cues, and underlying emotions. By understanding their perspective and needs, you can respond more effectively and build rapport. This skill helps create a positive negotiation environment and fosters a collaborative approach. Someone does not want to pay the bill because their baby is sick. People are going to reach for some heart wrenching excuses to wiggle out of paying you or delivering goods to you at the contract price.

Empathy and Emotional Intelligence: Empathy allows you to understand and share the feelings of others, while emotional intelligence enables you to manage your own emotions and navigate the emotions of others. Both skills are crucial in negotiation, as they help establish trust, manage conflicts, and find mutually beneficial solutions. Using your cool head and your onboard emotional intelligence is going to help resolve the matter. Emotional intelligence will help you decode the message the opponent is telling you, allowing you to explain how their story does not hold water.

Effective Communication: Strong communication skills are vital for negotiation success. This includes clearly articulating your own position, using persuasive language, and adapting your communication style to match the needs of the other party. Being able to convey your ideas effectively increases the likelihood of reaching mutually satisfying agreements.

Many conflicts are based on the state law in which you reside. You need to be sharp in contract law, labor law, and the law of torts to win in business. Many bookstores have summaries of each subject area of the law. University libraries are also a good source of legal information to build your knowledge and skills to avoid conflict and to understand the things your lawyer is warning you about when they talk about the hazards of your business and litigation exposure potential.

Problem Solving and Creativity: Negotiation often involves finding innovative solutions to complex problems. Possessing strong problem solving skills allows you to identify and address the underlying issues that may be hindering agreement. Being creative in exploring alternative options and proposing mutually beneficial compromises enhances the chances of reaching successful outcomes.

Resilience and Patience: Negotiations can be challenging and may involve setbacks or impasses. Resilience is the ability to bounce back from setbacks and maintain a positive attitude. Patience is crucial in negotiation, as rushing or being overly aggressive can harm the negotiation process. Both qualities help you persevere through difficult negotiations and maintain a long-term focus on achieving mutually beneficial results. It is to your advantage to show no anger and to not let your short temper fly. It is not the way toward resolution.

Remember that these skills are interconnected and work in tandem to enhance negotiation outcomes. Developing and honing these skills through practice and self-awareness can significantly improve a seasoned business owner's negotiating ability. The purpose of negotiation is to reach an agreement that is mutually advantageous/satisfactory to both parties.

Hiring and Team Building: Identify the key roles required for your business and hire talented individuals with the right skills and cultural fit. Clearly define job responsibilities, provide training, and foster a positive work environment.

Hiring talent is something very important to a business, just as is finding the right team players and teammates to staff a new NFL team for your city. Talent is the key to success. Hiring unskilled people may be fine for the production floor, but this is not the right choice for managers and job levels above managers. You want a star engineering staff, an all-pro marketing personnel, whiz kids as the accounting staff, and a top motivational speaker as your production chief. Talent, talent, talent is what your business needs.

Hiring and team building are vital for the success of a new entrepreneurial business. A strong team can bring diverse skills, experiences, and perspectives, fostering innovation and creativity.

By carefully selecting talented individuals, the business can enhance productivity and achieve goals efficiently. Additionally, a cohesive team creates a positive work culture, fostering collaboration and motivation.

Effective team building improves communication, trust, and morale, leading to increased employee satisfaction and retention. Ultimately, investing in hiring and team building ensures a solid foundation for growth and prosperity in the competitive business landscape. On your team you will have diverse personalities make sure everyone understands their job on the team and make sure they do their job and stay in their lane.

Launch and Adapt: Execute your business plan, launch your product or service, and start serving customers. Monitor your progress, gather feedback, and adapt your strategies as needed. Stay agile and open to changes and innovations.

Launch is the step where you have your location all set up to receive customers. You have made arrangements with the local Chamber of Commerce to hold a ribbon cutting ceremony. You open the doors and invite the customers in. From this activity and interaction, you can begin to see what works and what is not working so well. Then, you make plans to adjust and improve until all is working well.

Remember, starting a new business is a dynamic process, and these steps provide a broad framework. Seek guidance from mentors and industry experts, continuously educate yourself, and remain resilient in the face of challenges.

There is emphasis on the importance of the launch of a business. The "launch and adapt" phase is a very busy phase in business beginnings for new entrepreneurial businesses.

Launching refers to taking action and bringing the business idea into the market. It is a crucial step because it allows entrepreneurs to test their assumptions, gain valuable feedback from the marketplace, and eventually validate their business model. Launching early enables entrepreneurs to capitalize on market opportunities and establish an early mover advantage over slow moving competition.

However, launching alone is not sufficient for success. Adaptation is equally vital. The entrepreneurial landscape is dynamic, and unforeseen challenges are bound to arise. By adopting a mindset of "continuous adaptation," entrepreneurs can quickly respond to market feedback, adjust their strategies, and improve their products or services. This flexibility allows them to stay ahead of the competition, meet customer demands effectively, and ensure long-term viability.

By instilling the "launch and adapt" approach, the goal is to empower entrepreneurs to embrace experimentation, learn from failures, and iterate their business model iteratively. This mindset fosters resilience, innovation, and the ability to navigate the ever changing entrepreneurial landscape.

The iterative process is the practice of building, refining, and improving a project, product, or initiative. Teams that use the iterative development process create, test, and revise until they're satisfied with the end result.

You will want to start your business, and every 90 days, take a comprehensive look at what is happening. Are the customers satisfied? Did you seek their feedback? Do you have a system for generating or inviting new customers to the business? Do you have sound systems and procedures, well defined roles for the employees, and an established chain of command? Are you making good decisions leading to more business over the next six months?

There is no time for paralysis. If you begin to feel overwhelmed, be sure that you, the business owner, the visionary, are on track to continue the growth of the company and not bogged down with where to put the inventory.

It is easy to get sidetracked; you may feel overwhelmed-- deal with it, and continue to lead the company while focused on the next 90-day goal. Over time, your well placed systems and procedures will kick in, and the feeling of being overwhelmed will simmer down. Don't get lost in the commotion associated with the startup phase of the business. Stay laser focused on growing the business and meeting your short-term and long-term targets.

Here is a pro football coach's take on the grit and determination you need to start, launch, and grow your business.

As a professional football coach, I've learned that success on the field doesn't come easy. It takes a relentless focus on your goals, a well structured game plan, and the ability to adapt and make quick decisions. These principles apply not only to football but also to starting a new business. If you want to succeed, you need to stay focused on your goals and ensure that all departments in your business function correctly.

Like a football team, a business comprises different departments that need to work together seamlessly. Each department plays a crucial role in the success of the overall organization. Building a strong team and ensuring each member understands their responsibilities and how their role contributes to the bigger picture is important. Encourage open communication, collaboration, and a shared sense of purpose to create a winning culture.

In any business, marketing is the engine that drives growth and development. It's like the offensive game plan in football, setting the tone and attracting customers. Invest in a solid marketing strategy, understand your target audience, and create compelling messages that resonate with them. Utilize various marketing channels to reach your audience and constantly analyze the data to make informed decisions.

However, it's crucial to remember that marketing alone cannot guarantee success. Just as a football team needs a strong defense to complement its offense, your business needs well-functioning departments across the board. Operations, finance, human resources, and customer service are all vital pieces of the puzzle. Each department must be aligned with the overall vision and work together efficiently to ensure the smooth functioning of the business.

In conclusion, starting a new business requires the same focus and determination as leading a pro team. Stay focused on your goals, ensure all departments function correctly, and let marketing lead the way to growth and development. By building a strong team, implementing effective strategies, and fostering a winning culture, you'll be well on your way to achieving success in your business endeavors.

## CHAPTER 15

# Being an Entrepreneur

Being an entrepreneur is a wonderful life experience that offers countless benefits and opportunities. It is a path allowing individuals to unleash their creativity, pursue their passions, and shape their destiny. While the journey of entrepreneurship may be challenging at times, the rewards and personal growth that come with it make it an incredibly fulfilling and exciting endeavor. To see your earnings become more than three times what you made at your 8 to 5 job. This makes you smile at the end of the day.

Being self-employed offers a range of advantages that many individuals find appealing. Here are the top seven benefits of being self-employed:

1. **Freedom and Independence:** One of the most frequently cited benefits of self-employment is the ability to make decisions on your own without the constraints of a boss or corporate policy.

You can chart your own course, decide which projects to take on, and determine the direction of your business.

2. **Flexible Work Hours:** Self-employment often allows individuals to choose when they work. This can be especially beneficial for people with families, other commitments, or those who simply work best at non-traditional hours.

3. **Potential for Unlimited Income:** Unlike traditional jobs where your salary might be fixed, being self-employed gives you the chance to earn based on your performance and the success of your business. If your business does well, your income has the potential to grow substantially.

4. **Personal Satisfaction:** There's a great sense of achievement in knowing that you've built something from the ground up. Every success feels personal, and there's a direct correlation between the effort you put in and the rewards you receive.

5. **Tax Advantages:** In many countries, self-employed individuals can benefit from tax deductions that aren't available to traditional employees. This can include deductions for home offices, business related expenses, travel, meals and more.

6. **Direct Control Over Work Environment:** As a self-employed individual, you have the flexibility to design your workspace the way you want it. Whether you prefer a home office, co-working space, or some other environment, the choice is yours. This can greatly enhance work satisfaction and productivity.

7. **Ability to Choose Clients and Projects:** Unlike employees who often have projects assigned to them, self-employed professionals can choose which clients to work with and which projects to take on. This can lead to more fulfilling and enjoyable work.

Here are several reasons why being an entrepreneur is such a wonderful life experience.

## Pursuing Passion and Purpose

One of the greatest advantages of being an entrepreneur is the ability to work on something that truly excites and motivates you. As an entrepreneur, you have the freedom to pursue your passions and align your work with your purpose in life. This level of fulfillment and satisfaction is often difficult to achieve in traditional employment settings.

## Creative Expression

Entrepreneurship provides an outlet for creative expression. Whether you are starting a business, inventing a new product, or solving a problem in a unique way, being an entrepreneur allows you to think outside the box and bring your ideas to life. The freedom to innovate and create is exhilarating and can lead to groundbreaking discoveries and developments.

## Independence and Freedom

Being your own boss and having control over your work is a liberating experience. Entrepreneurs have the autonomy to make decisions, set their own schedules, and determine the direction of their businesses. This level of independence allows for flexibility and the ability to prioritize personal and professional goals according to one's own values. You can factor into your calendar when you are going to the beach, playing golf, playing tennis, nature hiking, riding your bike, going to the gym, or sleeping in!

## Personal Growth and Learning

Entrepreneurship is a journey of continuous personal growth and learning. As you navigate the challenges and obstacles that come with starting and running a business, you develop valuable skills such as problem solving, decision making, adaptability, and resilience while staying in touch with your determination. The entrepreneurial journey pushes you to step out of your comfort zone and develop a growth mindset, ultimately leading to personal and professional development.

## Impact and Influence

Entrepreneurs have the power to make a significant impact on the world around them. By introducing new products, services, or solutions, entrepreneurs have the potential to improve lives, disrupt industries, and contribute to positive social change. The ability to create something meaningful and leave a lasting legacy is a powerful motivator for many entrepreneurs.

## Financial Rewards

While financial success is not guaranteed in entrepreneurship, it is a possibility. Building a successful business can lead to financial independence and wealth creation. As an entrepreneur, you have the opportunity to control your income and potentially earn more than you would in a traditional job. However, it is important to note that financial rewards should not be the sole motivation for becoming an entrepreneur, as the journey requires dedication, hard work, and perseverance. If you work at your business and master it, you will be able to climb high with rewarding earnings.

## Building Network and Community

Entrepreneurship provides opportunities to connect and collaborate with like-minded individuals. Building a network of mentors, partners, and fellow entrepreneurs can provide invaluable support, guidance, and opportunities for growth. Additionally, being part of a vibrant entrepreneurial community can inspire and motivate you to reach new heights.

Being an entrepreneur is a wonderful life experience that offers countless benefits. It allows individuals to pursue their passions, unleash their creativity, and shape their own destiny. The journey of entrepreneurship is filled with personal growth, independence, and the opportunity to make a positive impact on the world. While it requires dedication and hard work, the rewards and fulfillment that come with being an entrepreneur make it a truly rewarding and exciting endeavor. I wish you all the best in your entrepreneurial pursuits.

While American universities offer prestigious and highly regarded entrepreneurship programs, there are still areas that could be enhanced to better serve individuals who own privately owned companies. Here are a few aspects that could be helpful:

1. **Practical Application:** Many entrepreneurship programs focus on theoretical knowledge and case studies. While this is valuable, incorporating more hands-on, practical applications would be beneficial. Practical exercises, real-world simulations, and opportunities to work directly with entrepreneurs and industry professionals can provide valuable insights and skills applicable to privately owned companies.

2. **Customization:** Privately owned companies often face unique challenges and opportunities compared to startups or publicly traded firms. Offering customized tracks or modules within entrepreneurship programs that cater specifically to the needs of privately owned companies would be valuable. This could include topics such as succession planning, family business dynamics, long-term sustainability, and managing growth in a private setting. Also, how to actively manage a growth company.

3. **Mentorship and Networking:** While many entrepreneurship programs provide access to mentors and networking opportunities, a focus on connecting participants with experienced entre-

preneurs who have successfully owned and operated private companies would be particularly beneficial. These mentors can offer practical advice, share their experiences, and provide guidance specific to privately owned businesses.

4. **Financial Resources:** Privately owned companies may have different financial needs and challenges compared to startups or publicly traded companies. Incorporating modules on topics such as alternative financing options, debt management, tax planning, and wealth preservation strategies would be valuable for entrepreneurs in this space. As well as retirement planning, net worth building, and ways to attract private party and private equity financing.

5. **Flexibility:** Many privately owned company owners have commitments and responsibilities that make participating in full-time or rigidly structured programs challenging. Offering flexible scheduling options, part-time programs, online courses, on demand courses or executive education programs specifically tailored for privately owned company owners can make education more accessible and feasible for busy entrepreneurs.

6. **Industry Focus:** Providing entrepreneurship programs that focus on specific industries relevant to privately owned companies can be helpful. For example, programs tailored to healthcare, manufacturing, farming, restaurants, wineries, technology, software development, retail or service based businesses can address industry-specific challenges, regulations, and best practices.

7. **Peer-to-Peer Learning:** Encouraging peer-to-peer learning and collaboration among participants who own privately owned companies can be valuable. Facilitating forums, group projects, or peer mentoring opportunities where participants can learn from each other's experiences and share insights specific to their businesses can enhance the educational experience. Breakout groups for regional CEOs or another group for regional CTOs or marketing executives and meeting, exchanging information, and making personal connections could be valuable. Universities talk about their connection to businesses and industry. Here is a way to be the sponsor of connecting the dots.

It's important to note that while Ivy League universities may not currently offer all of these elements in their entrepreneurship programs, there are other institutions, business associations, and professional development programs that focus specifically on the needs of privately owned companies. Exploring these options can provide additional resources and support for entrepreneurs in this space.

There are numerous reasons why a person might choose to put time, effort, and passion into starting a new business as an entrepreneur. Here are some common motivations:

1. **Pursuit of a Passion:** Many individuals have a strong desire to turn their passion into a career. Starting a business allows them to build something around their interests and dedicate themselves to work they genuinely enjoy. Work can become a want-to rather than a have-to!

2. **Independence and Autonomy:** Entrepreneurship offers the opportunity to be your own boss and have control over your work life and career development. This autonomy can be highly appealing, especially for individuals who prefer a more self-directed approach to work.

3. **Financial Potential:** Starting a successful business can provide significant financial rewards. Entrepreneurs often have the potential to earn more than they would in traditional employment. Additionally, building a business allows individuals to create wealth and financial security for themselves and their families.

4. **Desire for Personal Growth:** Starting a business is a challenging and dynamic journey that requires continuous learning and personal development. Many people are drawn to the opportunity for growth, both in terms of acquiring new skills and expanding their knowledge. They also understand that there is the potential for their salary to surpass regular employment opportunities.

5. **Flexibility and Work-Life Balance:** Being an entrepreneur can provide greater flexibility in terms of working hours and location. This flexibility allows individuals to design their work-life balance according to their preferences and priorities. Having a spiritual life, family life, outdoor activity life, travel life, relationships life, work life, continuing education life. There are many sectors of your life that need time and attention.

6. **Creating a Legacy:** Some individuals are driven by the desire to leave a lasting impact on the world. Starting a business provides an avenue for building something meaningful, contributing to their community or industry, and leaving a legacy for future generations.

7. **Dissatisfaction with Traditional Employment:** Some people may feel unfulfilled or constrained in their current jobs and desire a change. They may be seeking a new challenge or want to escape the limitations of corporate structures. Many people desire to get paid for what they do.

8. **Recognition and Status:** Building a successful business can lead to recognition and status within the industry or community. This can be a motivating factor for individuals who aspire to be known for their accomplishments and expertise.

9. **Solving a Problem or Meeting a Need:** Entrepreneurs often identify gaps in the market or have innovative solutions to existing problems. They may be driven by a desire to create a product or service that improves people's lives or addresses an unmet need.

10. **Long-term Vision:** Some individuals have a long-term vision of creating a business that will provide stability, financial freedom, and fulfillment in the future. They are willing to put in the effort and sacrifice in the early stages to achieve their vision later on.

Of course, each individual's motivations can vary based on their unique circumstances, experiences, and personal aspirations. Starting a business is a significant undertaking, and the reasons for doing so can be a combination of multiple motivating factors.

Getting your spouse's consent and support when embarking on a self-employment journey is crucial for a strong foundation and a successful business. Here are some steps to help you gain their understanding, agreement and support:

1. **Open Communication:** Initiate an open and honest conversation with your spouse. Clearly express your aspirations, goals, and reasons for wanting to become self-employed. Discuss your vision, the potential benefits, and the challenges you might face. Encourage them to share their thoughts and concerns. Ask them if they are willing to support your efforts. Its fair to tell them that life as the routine that it has been will be changing, but in the big picture of things soon life will be way better once the business is launched and underway.

2. **Address Concerns:** Be prepared to address any reservations or fears your spouse may have. Understand their perspective and empathize with their worries about financial stability or uncertainty. Address each concern with a realistic plan, including a backup strategy and financial projections to alleviate their worries. Some of their worries may come from true concern and some may be coming from selfishness. Its up to you to decern the difference, then ask for the cooperation.

3. **Share Your Research:** Demonstrate your commitment and dedication by presenting a well-researched business plan. Show how you have studied the market, identified opportunities, and developed a strategy for success. Share success stories of others who have achieved self-employment, highlighting the potential rewards. Explain the technical things and don't pitch this the way you would to a room full of VC's, pitch this to your life partner!

4. **Financial Planning:** Assure your spouse that you have considered the financial implications and have a solid plan in place. Discuss your budget, savings, and any potential sources of income during the initial stages of the business. Develop a timeline for achieving financial stability and share it with your spouse. Borrowing against the equity of your house would supply the necessary capital to start the business.

5. **Involve Them in the Process:** Invite your spouse to be a part of your entrepreneurial journey. Encourage them to share their insights, opinions, and ideas. Involve them in decision making processes, such as choosing a business name or designing a logo. Their involvement will foster a sense of ownership and increase their support.

6. **Seek Compromise:** Be open to compromise and find a balance between your entrepreneurial ambitions and your spouse's needs.

Discuss and set realistic expectations for your work-life balance, especially during the initial stages of the business. Assure your spouse that their needs and well-being remain a priority.

7. **Reassure With a Backup Plan:** While embarking on any entrepreneurial venture involves risks, present a backup plan to alleviate concerns. Identify alternative options or part-time opportunities that can provide a safety net during challenging times. This will provide your spouse with a sense of security. Explain to the spouse if they secure and maintain a job with an employer that has benefits and health insurance coverage, when the business gets up and running, they may quit their job and return to raising the children if they desire this.

8. **Show Commitment:** Demonstrate your dedication and commitment to making the self-employment venture successful. This includes working diligently, staying motivated, and continuously communicating your progress to your spouse. Show that you are willing to put in the necessary effort to make the business thrive.

Being an entrepreneur is a wonderful life experience that offers countless benefits and opportunities. It is a path allowing individuals to unleash their creativity, pursue their passions, and shape their destiny.

Remember, gaining your spouse's consent and support may take time. Be patient, understanding, and receptive to their concerns. Addressing their doubts and fears with empathy and a well-thought-out plan will increase the likelihood of obtaining their support as you embark on this potentially bumpy journey together.

Entrepreneurs continue to face various challenges. Here are some of the most difficult problems entrepreneurs may encounter:

1. **Market Competition:** The business landscape is highly competitive, and entrepreneurs need to find ways to differentiate their products or services from others in the market. Standing out and capturing market share can be a significant challenge.

2. **Rapid Technological Advancements:** Technology evolves at a fast pace, and entrepreneurs must adapt to keep up with the latest trends. Incorporating new technologies into their business operations, such as artificial intelligence, blockchain, or automation, while ensuring their business remains relevant can be daunting.

3. **Talent Acquisition and Retention:** Finding and retaining skilled employees is a perennial challenge for entrepreneurs. In a competitive job market, attracting talented individuals with the right skill sets becomes increasingly difficult, especially for startups and small businesses with limited resources.

4. **Funding and Financing:** Accessing adequate funding to start or scale a business can be a major hurdle. Entrepreneurs often face difficulties in securing loans, finding investors, or obtaining venture capital. Economic conditions, market volatility, and stringent lending practices can further complicate the funding process.

5. **Regulatory and Legal Compliance:** Navigating complex legal and regulatory frameworks is a challenge for entrepreneurs. Compliance with laws related to taxation, intellectual property, data privacy, safety protocol and industry specific regulations adds a layer of complexity to business operations.

6. **Changing Consumer Behavior:** Consumer preferences and behaviors constantly evolve, and entrepreneurs must adapt accordingly. Understanding and meeting the ever changing demands of consumers, as well as keeping up with emerging trends, can pose significant challenges.

7. **Sustainable Practices:** As environmental concerns continue to grow, entrepreneurs face the challenge of adopting sustainable practices. Meeting sustainability goals while maintaining profitability and operational efficiency can be a delicate balancing act.

8. **Cybersecurity and Data Privacy:** With increasing digitalization, entrepreneurs must prioritize cybersecurity and protect sensitive customer data. The threat of cyber attacks, data breaches, and regulatory penalties necessitates robust security measures, which can be complex and expensive to implement. Robust security is important. What you put in "the cloud" should be carefully done while considering what data to keep solely in-house for privacy and security reasons.

9. **Scaling and Growth:** Successfully scaling a business while maintaining quality standards and customer satisfaction is a major challenge for entrepreneurs. Managing growth related issues such as operational scalability, supply chain management, and expanding into new markets can be demanding.

10. **Economic Uncertainty:** Economic factors, such as market volatility, inflation, interest rates, and geopolitical instability, can impact entrepreneurs' ability to plan for growth and forecast effectively. Uncertainty in the economic landscape adds an additional layer of complexity to business decision making.

It's important to note that the challenges faced by entrepreneurs can vary depending on factors such as industry, location, business size, and individual circumstances.

Self-employed people are able to enjoy more things in life and have experiences in their early years, they thought were unimaginable. Self-employed people enjoy the benefits of choosing their activities, longer and more frequent vacations, to high end resorts, more family time, share more quality experiences with their children. Self-employed people have more time for hobbies, sports and passions and of course business travel. Self-employed people if you look around own airplanes, yachts, expensive jewelry, go shopping, own second and third homes, sporty automobiles. So, if you enjoy finer things and want your salary to increase then join the growing ranks of the self-employed.

We are here to encourage and guide you on your journey. We are also here for already developed companies that need a push to get to the next level. Set a target for your business and do not settle for average, or we got it started, then sat down with contentment and did not make an effort to move to the next level.

Self-employment comes with so much satisfaction, freedom, and joy that people who have experienced this would never return to the 8 to 5 jobs. They enjoy the freedom and flexibility that self-employment brings. Start your business and reach for the top of the mountain. Don't give up, give in, or let go. Continue to climb, soar, and achieve your dreams. Go down in history as the best there is, the best there ever was, and the best there ever will be.

Don't forget that part of being an entrepreneur is to get your spouse's consent to the ride and support toward your accomplishments. There are two other noteworthy books that I have written, "Money and Marriage for Engaged Couples" and Money and Marriage-Making it Work Together."

To contact us for management consulting engagements:

Canberra Company,

Post Office Box 23209

Santa Barbara, California 93121.

Contact phone is 805.962.1040,

email to info@canberracompanytax.com.

Write and tell me inspirational stories about your leap into entrepreneurship and some of the bumps along the way!

# The End

In closing, it's up to you to put yourself in a position to overcome the psychological barriers that prevent people from joining the forces of the self-employed. Self-employment has its rewards, and it is worth the leap.

Believe in yourself, and make the decision to gain your freedom and independence. Let go of the limiting beliefs. Believe in your own abilities to plan and organize a business that you will become proud of. Stand up and make a difference. Embrace self-confidence and exercise your self-starter abilities. Know with brimming confidence that you are a special talent. Improve your self-talk, and from your inner self, possess the strong beliefs that: "I think I can" I think I can" then know that…. "YOU CAN."

Surround yourself with people who can help, push, invest, and support your efforts. Plan to learn more about the different facets of your business and industry. Become a leader and guide your employees so they feel at home, part of the family, and able to help you meet your goals.

At all times, stay within the law and keep the tax collector happy, the banker paid, and your spouse satisfied.

Become prepared, make the leap, keep growing, and call me when your sales exceed $500 million.

# Index

## A

Accounting  40, 42, 73, 102, 151
advanced entrepreneur  136
Amassing Wealth  93

## B

balance sheet  9, 72, 73, 74, 76
Balance Sheet  73, 107
Banking Relationship  67
belief system  83, 86
benefits programs  55
Builder  11, 12
business acumen  100
business broker  21, 199, 202
business plan  12, 16, 23, 24, 25, 28, 79, 122, 123, 124, 125, 193, 196, 217, 218, 219, 220, 233, 234, 235, 253, 254, 255, 259, 269, 284
business strategy  27, 47

## C

Canberra Company  iii, 134, 138, 288
career path  81, 82
cash flow  9, 38, 42, 70, 71, 72, 73, 76, 111, 126, 147, 158, 204, 223, 236
cash flow statement  71, 72, 73, 76
Chamber of Commerce  31, 129, 270
choice of entity  264
Competition  9, 285
Cost of Goods Sold  6, 76
CPI  117
Credibility  69
credit score  73, 105
critical decisions  34, 223
crowdfunding  27, 215, 233, 234, 236
customer satisfaction  38, 39, 44, 50, 59, 60, 127, 141, 143, 157, 158, 160, 186, 187, 188, 190, 203, 266, 287
Cybersecurity  287

## D

delegate  37, 40, 63, 91, 92, 193
depreciation  41, 75, 76, 247, 248
determination  81, 112, 121, 135, 167, 255, 258, 259, 271, 273, 278
DJIA  116
due diligence  80, 186, 199, 201, 226, 260

## E

economic forecasts  114
economics  113, 115, 116, 119, 257
employee handbook  39, 56, 101
entrepreneurial mindset  13, 258
EQ  157, 175
execution  12, 16, 28, 88, 124, 125, 154, 155, 188, 255, 259, 261

## F

family business  139, 140, 279
Federal Reserve  114
Financial Management  9, 50
financial performance  70, 76, 77, 78
financial reports  40, 42, 106
franchisee  17, 18

## G

GDP  30, 117
Generally Accepted Accounting Principles  73
gross profit  40, 51, 75, 76, 242, 245, 246, 247, 248

## H

high achievers 83, 85

## I

I-9 Form 54
Income Statement 73, 74
incubators 28
insurance 3, 55, 60, 104, 105, 106, 138, 146, 149, 229, 237, 242, 248, 285
Inventory 52, 107, 151
Investor 15, 77, 212, 249
IPO 126, 211, 225, 226
IQ 158, 175
IRS 106, 118

## J

jingle 259

## L

labor law firms 54
labor laws 16, 54, 55, 56, 252, 256
Launching 270
leadership iii, 3, 11, 46, 88, 90, 91, 120, 139, 140, 145, 152, 153, 154, 155, 156, 157, 159, 160, 162, 167, 172, 176, 206, 224, 243, 244
Leadership Skills 90
lines of credit 114, 216, 234

## M

made in America 115, 127
managing wealth 93
market analysis 8, 124, 125
Mentor 15
mentorship 145, 159, 165, 217, 236
merger and acquisition 57
multi-unit 143, 144, 145

## N

Negotiation Skills 267
net profit 41, 75, 200, 242, 243, 248, 249, 250
Net Profit 41, 77, 242
networking 25, 31, 39, 69, 91, 130, 131, 132, 133, 134, 135, 171, 232, 236, 258, 279
NFIB 31, 129

## O

operational framework. 63
Operations Manager 16
organizational chart 82, 192, 193, 263

## P

passion 2, 85, 88, 97, 181, 255, 258, 259, 281
payroll 3, 39, 54, 55, 56, 57, 61, 69, 72, 100, 101, 106, 120, 151, 256
prime rate 114
private equity 68, 103, 157, 160, 188, 196, 210, 212, 213, 222, 224, 225, 226, 228, 229, 231, 262, 264, 280
Production 63
Profit and Loss Statement 107
public relations 3, 44, 45, 61, 62, 63, 120, 243
Purchasing agents 51, 52

## Q

quality control 58, 59, 60, 61, 119, 120, 245

## R

Record Retention 60
risk management 50, 52, 252
Risk Management 9, 50, 70, 210
risks 4, 7, 8, 9, 10, 15, 50, 52, 70, 80, 120, 164, 187, 188, 191, 195, 201, 210, 212, 217, 223, 224, 238, 239, 250, 252, 258, 285

## S

sales funnel 25
SBA 29, 30, 68, 109, 111, 146, 211, 234, 235

Self-Awareness  81, 89
self-employment  i, ii, 2, 7, 24, 27, 83,
    84, 85, 86, 97, 111, 121, 122, 163,
    181, 202, 275, 283, 284, 285, 288
self-help  86, 87, 88, 89, 90, 91, 173
self-improvement  86, 121
SEO  27
stages  25, 27, 38, 45, 86, 103, 118, 193,
    194, 212, 213, 218, 219, 224, 228,
    230, 283, 284
start-up  22, 27, 44, 45, 46, 47, 78, 79,
    80, 88, 122, 165, 196, 205, 218,
    219, 228, 260
statement of income  75, 76, 78
strategic planning  iii, 8, 12, 78, 90, 144,
    145, 206, 247, 261, 263
Strategist  16
succession planning  iii, 104, 138, 139,
    140, 141, 193, 263, 279
Supply and Demand  119
supply chain  16, 52, 117, 222, 238, 246,
    252, 266, 287

## T

Talent  269, 286
team building  iii, 32, 33, 34, 35, 120,
    151, 269
technology  30, 39, 107, 126, 142, 151,
    152, 184, 190, 210, 216, 223, 224,
    228, 230, 232, 238, 262, 265, 266,
    280
Time Management  10, 91
Trust  35, 98

## U

Unemployment rate  117
uniformity  17, 18, 148, 222
uniqueness  2, 139, 153

## V

valuation  136, 200, 202, 213, 216, 217,
    250
venture capital  27, 28, 68, 78, 79, 80,
    122, 124, 125, 126, 160, 196, 212,
    213, 214, 215, 219, 220, 221, 226,
    227, 228, 229, 230, 231, 232, 236,
    264, 286
Visualization  177

## W

W4 Form  54
wealth accumulation  93, 94, 95
Working Capital  210

## Z

zero based budgeting  189

# ORDER FORM

This order form should be used to order books to send to your family and friends that are self-employed. If you own a business you will want to order a book for your employees so that you are all running your company by being in the same page.

**Fax orders :** 805-421-4767

**Telephone Orders:** 1-805-962-1040

**Address for postal orders:**

Abundance Publishing Company
Post Office Box 23209
Santa Barbara, California 93121
Web site: growmybusiness.help

## Print your name and shipping address:

Name_____

Address _____

City    _____      State  _____Zip
_____ Your Telephone Number_____

**Entrepreneurship-Believe and Achieve**

_____ Quantity of books @ $22.95 _____

Sales Tax for Your County or 8.5% _____

Shipping & Handling $7.00 _____

Federal Express: 25.00 _____

**Total** _____

Payment: _____Check Enclosed _____ Credit Card

Type of Card: ❏ Visa ❏ Mastercard

Name on Card _____

Address _____

City_____State_____Zip_____

Card Number _____ Expires _____

Authorized Signature _____

_____ Would you like information on the next Entrepreneurship Seminar/Webinar

www.ingramcontent.com/pod-product-compliance
Lightning Source LLC
Chambersburg PA
CBHW062056290426
44110CB00022B/2615